One Kind
of
Knowing

REPORTS FROM A
HALLUCINOGEN
RESEARCH VOLUNTEER

Maria Estevez

ISBN 978-0-9859545-2-9

I wish to express my thanks to my
sisters Lisa and Alida and my brother Lance
for taking me to my appointments at Johns Hopkins.
I am also grateful to Jane Orfgen, Carolyn Gibbs,
and Valerie Weis for their personal support
and comments on the manuscript.

TABLE OF CONTENTS

Introduction

The Johns Hopkins University School of Medicine — a name that evokes gravity, responsibility, and esteem. Its reputation for treatment and research is unsurpassed. Yet beyond this traditional agenda some remarkable investigations into the effect of drugs on mind and body are being conducted as part of the Psilocybin Research Project at its Behavioral Pharmacology Research Unit in Baltimore, Maryland.

After a hiatus of thirty years, when hallucinogens like LSD were ruled illegal due to the drug excesses of the 1960s, these mind-altering compounds are once again the subject of serious study at a number of research facilities. Investigators at Harvard University, the University of California (Harbor UCLA), the University of Arizona, and New York University, for example, are exploring therapeutic applications for conditions such as obsessive-compulsive disorder and substance abuse, and to provide insights and comfort to cancer patients. Some of the more physiological research has been conducted in Germany and Switzerland with healthy volunteers.

Johns Hopkins was among the leaders in reinitiating human hallucinogen research in the U.S., and its first study on humans (2000-2006) was the most experimentally rigorous blinded study with these substances to date. Perhaps more significantly, the programs at Johns Hopkins are the only research with hallucinogens using measures of spirituality as one of the primary endpoints. Dr. Bill Richards, who co-authored the first study there, had been involved in some of the best clinical work with hallucinogens during the 1960s and 1970s. The program's principal researcher for these projects, Dr. Roland Griffiths, had distinguished himself as a leading psychopharmacologist, and his laboratory was already approved to work with controlled substances before the studies were proposed.

Encouraged by the critical success of their first study, a second was begun in 2005, funded by grants from the Council on Spiritual Practices, the Heffter Research Institute, the Betsy Gordon Foundation, and the National Institutes of Health. Eighteen volunteers were chosen from 279 phone screenings and subsequent interviews to ingest four varying doses of psilocybin (the active ingredient in "magic" mushrooms, which had been chemically synthesized) with careful preparation, supervision, and follow-up. The staff has gathered valuable new data from the study that has been presented at scientific meetings and published in scholarly journals. But my account is offered from a different perspective — I had the privilege of participating as one of the volunteers.

I had not taken hallucinogens before joining the program, and had little information about them to guide or to prejudice me, so I approached the psilocybin sessions with almost no preconceptions. My reaction to the strong initial dose nearly caused me to withdraw from the program, but in my second session I was opened to a profound mystical experience that will remain a lifelong treasure. Two subsequent lower doses also brought moving responses.

When I agreed to join the study it was not my intention to write about the procedures or my reactions. But as I continued through the application process, the preparation and the actual sessions, I realized that a report could be helpful to others in the medical and spiritual communities. The chapters here cover my activities during the program and over the next several years until the final results of the study were announced in 2011. Conversations are approximate, but all the events are documented.

My staff guides invited me to describe my perceptions during the six to eight hours of each psilocybin session. I am naturally inclined to observe, interpret and record, so that is what I began to do from the first moments I felt an effect. Besides the reports that were required the day after a session, I wrote additional passages in my journals, so the narrative here draws from fresh impressions, not reconstructions. Rereading them even now brings me back to the immediacy and emotional tone of the original moment. The routine questionnaires always asked whether I'd ever had an experience that could not be expressed in words. I'd grin and tell the staff, "You know I'm going to give it a try!"

These circumstances manifested in my life in such a singular manner and affected me so deeply that they could not have been accidental or coincidental. I write with a yearning to craft something tangible as a testament and an expression of gratitude. It is also my hope that this outline of the thorough design of the project and a description of the kind of alterations in consciousness possible with psilocybin will promote further research. If this can serve as an illustration, then the world is welcome to it. As the Sufis pray, "May I contribute to the transformation of the universe."

I cherish the joy of having reached a transcendental state of consciousness, though it was with the assistance of a hallucinogen. Countless others, living and dead, famous and obscure, have reached such levels through their own attunement and discipline or as a spontaneous revelation. At this moment many are sitting in deep communion in ashrams, abbeys, garrets and huts, expanded into higher dimensions and translating the energy into a shared human resource. The brief, temporary access I experienced gives me the greatest respect for those who have established such an intimate union with the Divine.

My interest in religion, metaphysics, and spirituality goes back as far as I can remember. This path has been a winding one, but my sincerity and intention have never wavered. I believe that we are all on a journey to God-realization, and I am grateful for being guided to take the scenic route.

CHAPTER ONE

Forty Years Late

It is unusual to be able to trace a life-changing adventure to its moment of origin, but I remember clearly just how this began. Then again, there was little about it that was *not* unusual.

One winter night I was relaxing at home on an extended Christmas holiday. My two cats were dozing. The 2006 New Year was only a few days old, and I was happy to think that after this year's birthday I could retire from my job.

I live alone and I live quietly, usually without either music or TV. There was always something around the house that needed to be done, but having caught up on my sleep after my long commute to work, I was thinking about plans for an art project that evening. I remembered Aldous Huxley's observation that every culture has valued precious stones, sparkling glass, shells, flowers, and brilliantly colored ornaments because they remind us of magical realms usually reached only in visions or dreams. Artists can captivate us with those same effects, he wrote. Huxley had made the case so articulately that I scanned my bookshelves looking for that citation. I picked up a volume with two of his best-known essays, but while trying to locate the reference, which I later found in *Heaven and Hell*, I became distracted with the account of his mescaline experience in *The Doors of Perception*.

It was easy to understand many of Huxley's reactions while he was in an altered state, such as his amusement at the sight of metal fashioned into an automobile. But I also read of his surprise that the drapery folds which transfixed him already had been appreciated by painters and sculptors through the centuries. I had admired those patterns too, and could stretch my imagination to other effects Huxley described, so I wondered how I would react to such a substance.

My acquaintance with that essay dated to the 1960s when I attended a small Catholic girls' college in the suburbs of New York. I was not one of the few students who challenged the strict rules. The drug culture may have been thriving elsewhere, but our campus was a model of decorum.

On only one occasion in my life had I stepped outside the boundaries. Soon after graduation, I spent the weekend with a smart, confident, and daring friend who offered me an opportunity to try marijuana. I'd told her my fantasies once when I was letting my mind wander.

"I was bored in class," I said, "leaning over the desk with my chin on my hands. My nose was only a few inches away from the girl in front of me, who was wearing a mohair sweater. I was gazing at the crinkly little fabric strands, and how much depth there was among them, and thinking that if I were only, say, an eighth of an inch tall I could climb in there and go exploring." My friend said, "With a mind like that, you don't need drugs!"

I remember this incident in particular because it was a rare occasion when I had shared one of my flights of fancy. After all the social and educational disciplines that had shaped my life, all the demands to conform, it was refreshing to think that a more imaginative attitude might not only be valued, but that there were even ways to promote it.

So when my friend rolled up some marijuana in delicate papers and offered it to me, I gave in to my curiosity. She had done this before, the setting seemed safe, and the effects were said to be mild. The only time I had ever tried smoking was a puff or two on my parents' cigarettes many years before, and I could not understand how anyone would purposely do something that tasted and felt so awful.

She instructed me to inhale the smoke and hold it as long as possible. With some concentration, I managed. Then she urged me to do it again, and again. It was unpleasant, but I wanted to find out for myself how reality might appear different. After about fifteen minutes, my throat was beginning to hurt but I felt no mood changes and saw no visual effects, so I decided not to continue. I had the same reaction when I tried it again the following day, so that became my excuse to quit, perhaps a little afraid that something unpredictable *would* occur. Thus began and ended my experimentation with recreational drugs.

As I reviewed Huxley's colorful description that January evening, I marveled at the possibility of altered perception and wished I too could have such an experience. But, just as during the first reading forty years earlier, I realized that I was much too conservative to risk taking hallucinogens unless I knew their strength or had supervision. Without such guidance, I found myself in the same rational loop as before, facing the same stalemate. But this time, the story would have a different ending.

The next day — the very next day, with Huxley's tale fresh in my mind — I was idly paging through a local magazine on alternative medical therapies and spiritual practices when I noticed a small display ad:

Seeking Persons Committed to Spiritual Development for a Study of States of Consciousness

Johns Hopkins University School of Medicine is seeking volunteers to participate in a scientific study of states of consciousness brought about by psilocybin, a psycho-active substance found in mushrooms and used sacra-mentally in some cultures. Volunteers will be carefully prepared and will be provided professional guidance before, during, and after five experimental sessions given in a pleasant, supportive setting.

Volunteers must be between the ages of 22 and 65, be in good physical health, have a four-year college degree, have no history of severe psychiatric illness or recent drug or alcohol abuse, and have an interest in spirituality.

For more information, please call [this phone number] and ask for Mary, the study's research coordinator. Confidentiality will be maintained for all applicants.

I was stunned. This could not have been a coincidence. It was as if divine providence had contrived to refresh my decades-old desire just before it set the fulfillment in front of my eyes. I had never heard of psilocybin, though I knew the excellent reputation of Johns Hopkins. I could hardly wait to contact them, but I worried that they would have so many applicants that I wouldn't stand a chance.

On the next business day I called to introduce myself to Mary. I briefly sketched my personal situation and my interest in the study. In turn, Mary explained that the program would extend over a six-month period for each volunteer. The psilocybin would be given in four doses: low, medium, medium-high, and high. Their order would be determined by a Johns Hopkins pharmacist using a table of random numbers and given to the volunteer "double-blind," meaning neither the guides nor the volunteer would know the dosage. That information would remain confidential until after the study was complete.

An initial screening of five or six hours was needed for psychological and medical testing, Mary said. A second screening of about three hours covered questionnaires and interviews. Volunteers who were accepted would have four preparatory meetings and five all-day sessions, about a month apart, when one of the four doses of psilocybin would be administered or the volunteer would receive a placebo during one session. Written reports and follow-up meetings were required after each session. Volunteers would not be allowed to drive home after the five sessions when psilocybin could be ingested, but must be picked up. After a volunteer's participation in the program was complete, a final appointment would be scheduled for a review one year later. There would be no financial compensation.

Mary told me that their staff had already completed one study on psilocybin with 36 volunteers who received no more than one dose each. For this second study there would be a total of 18 volunteers. Some were already in the process, but all positions were not yet filled.

"I would think you'd be deluged with volunteers for a study like this," I said.

"We thought so too," she replied, "but that hasn't been the case. Some people call once and we never hear from them again." Perhaps the requirements sounded a little more demanding than they expected.

Mary informed me the sessions were being held in Baltimore. When she asked where I lived, I described the location as within commuting distance of the Washington, D.C., suburbs, and said I didn't see a problem with making the trips to Baltimore. A number of the volunteers in the first study had come from the Washington area, Mary said. In truth, the drive sounded daunting, but I was willing to consider it.

I was also concerned about admitting I was 61, so I tried a little salesmanship to suggest that it might be of interest to have someone older in the study. I was assuming that young people would be likeliest to apply, but Mary said that most of their participants had been middle-aged.

During our discussion Mary asked for my height and weight. When I told her, she advised that according to their charts I was 20 pounds over the limit for my height. Adding the threat of disqualification to my own guilt on the issue was enough to prompt me into action. I took a deep breath and asked if I had time to improve that number and still join the program. I promised to call her again in a month with a good report.

From that moment, I adopted a strict regimen to meet the guidelines for the study. I could not find time to exercise — my commute to work didn't even allow me eight hours' sleep a night — so the weight loss would depend entirely on what I ate. For the next few months I eliminated every indulgence and monitored every calorie. Rather than following popular diets or joining a group, I had smaller portions and made better choices. These were obvious and sensible adjustments like giving up snacks in the car, butter on my toast, and apple pie in favor of the apple. I made sure to get a good balance of nutrients, and if I couldn't find a simple way to satisfy my hunger, I just tolerated it. I even bought a digital scale that marked the pounds in increments so I could keep close track of my progress. Perhaps more important, I did all this cheerfully and privately, with conviction I would succeed.

In early February, I called Mary again to say I had lost ten pounds toward my goal and was hoping a place was still available in the study. She was encouraging, so I continued my self-assigned discipline. A few weeks later I had a phone message from her that a quota of volunteers was scheduled at that time, and recruiting would resume in two to three months. She promised to keep my name on file. I was grateful for a little more time to trim down. They could find plenty of reasons to reject me, I thought, but it wasn't going to be those twenty pounds.

Meanwhile, my office was busy preparing for a conference, and I was already hinting that I wanted to retire soon after my birthday in April. I told my supervisor about my hope of joining the study because I might have to take off a day or two for appointments in Baltimore; otherwise, it seemed best not to discuss the matter.

As warm spring weather and the prospect of more leisure brought me a new sense of liberation, I decided to visit some of the ancient sacred sites in England. I signed up to join a tour scheduled for July, so it seemed reasonable to stay at my job a few more months.

Meeting the Researchers

More than six months after my initial contact with the researchers, at last Mary called to arrange an interview toward the end of June. I printed out directions to the address on the East side of Baltimore and got a full tank of gas. To make sure I arrived on time for my 9:30 a.m. appointment, I left the house at 6:30 that morning, and arrived with a half-hour to spare. The odometer registered 95 miles from door to door, almost all on major highways with a minimum of congestion.

The Johns Hopkins Bayview Campus was a jumble of utilitarian office buildings and parking lots. The Behavioral Pharmacology Research Unit I was seeking occupied one of the older buildings, where uniformed security guards buzzed open doors for the few visitors and also watched a bank of closed-circuit screens of the parking lots, sidewalks, doors and hallways. I later learned part of the building houses a court-mandated drug treatment program.

When Mary came down to the lobby to greet me, I finally had an image to associate with the voice that had become so familiar — she was petite with dark hair and a bright smile. Mary welcomed me and escorted me up to the third floor, a warren of small offices and cubicles with narrow hallways, dull carpet, and fluorescent lights. It was difficult to imagine that anything extraordinary could happen in such a setting.

The States of Consciousness study was staffed by Mary Cosimano, Dr. Matt Johnson, and Dr. Roland Griffiths. Mary also mentioned Dr. Bill Richards who had helped set up the protocols for the first study, and often worked from another location. She told me the results of that study were being prepared for public release in a few weeks.

After we talked for a few minutes, Mary invited me to

read over and sign a nine-page Consent Form before we began the interviews, disclosures, and examinations. Then she took me down to the second floor for a weigh-in. I expected to be within the range, but Mary's measurement of my height was a half-inch shorter than my estimate, so I was asked to lose a few more pounds for the new ratio.

I met with a staff physician and nurse, provided samples for bloodwork tests and even an HIV test, filled out a medical history, and got approval on my blood pressure reading. Female volunteers routinely receive a pregnancy test as well. Then, with Mary observing, I spent several hours in the office of another staffer providing oral answers for a series of standard psychological questionnaires that covered subjects like family health and history. (Did I ever feel a need to count up to a certain number? Before age 15, did I take things from people or set fires?)

When asked about my use of alcohol, I said there were only a few times in my life when I'd had too much to drink, the last one about 35 years before, and most of those consisted of just one mixed drink. Inebriation was not a feeling I liked, and an alcoholic parent was the only lesson I needed. Now I have no more than one glass of wine, perhaps several times a week.

There were extensive questions about any illicit drug use, where I answered no to a longer list of drugs than I could have thought to name on my own, including heroin, cocaine, crack, LSD, peyote, mescaline, psilocybin, hashish, opium, Ecstasy, amphetamines, methadone, crystal meth, speed, morphine, PCP, Valium, barbiturates, steroids, glue, inhalants, and nitrous oxide. Even though I told them about my single experiment with marijuana, my life sounded rather dull. I was a child of the '60s, but I had missed all the action. I admitted to a less-than-ideal relationship with my parents, to claustrophobia, a few bouts of depression, and to one brother having epilepsy, but that was as far as I varied from the norm. After the interview I remembered to tell Mary that I also had a touch of synesthesia, but hadn't heard any questions on it. "Oh, they were in there," she said, and repeated some subtle wording that had gone right over my head.

Mary took me down the hall to meet the personable Dr. Matt Johnson. In time I learned that he was 32, with a Ph.D. in Experimental Psychology, and had been on the staff for three years. Matt, as he invited me to call him, teamed with Mary as a monitor or guide during psilocybin sessions for some of the volunteers. His years of work in psychopharmacology included research on a variety of substances such as nicotine and cocaine, and he was knowledgeable about the history of drug usage. Matt explained that one of the reasons psilocybin was chosen was its six-to-eight-hour range, while mescaline such as Huxley used requires eight to twelve hours to run its course.

"Mushrooms, peyote and other natural substances have been used for centuries in many parts of the world for spiritual purposes," Matt told me. "But the native cultures have almost always taken them sacramentally, not recreationally." He clearly stated that the synthesized psilocybin used in this study, the active ingredient in "magic" mushrooms, was virtually non-addictive and non-toxic. Rather than being called hallucinogens or psychedelics, he said, these are now referred to as entheogens. I recognized the Greek root *theos,* and Matt confirmed that it was considered a "God-revealing" substance, and was respected for such properties by those indigenous societies.

The research team was looking for volunteers who were "hallucinogen-naïve," with minimal experience or preconceptions, but with a spiritual background to help them better interpret the effects.

After meeting with Matt, I returned to Mary's office to continue with my application, filling out multiple-choice forms on my views and experiences with a broad range of spiritual subjects. I was also asked to provide names and contact information for three friends or family members whom the researchers would interview by phone three times during the study for their assessment of my attitudes and behaviors. Mary informed me that separate appointments would be arranged with Dr. Richards and Dr. Griffiths. In the meantime my medical tests would be processed, and I had a few more pounds to lose. My copy of the Consent Form showed an assigned number in the box labeled "Patient I.D. Plate." I didn't have final approval yet, but the paperwork looked official. Even though I was pleased to have progressed to that point, I still didn't feel I could tell most of my family and friends about the program.

As I prepared to leave my job of eight years, I cleaned out my desk and made notes for my replacement. My office gave me a fine luncheon, and I knew I'd miss my coworkers, if not the traffic. One friend, who became employed again when boredom set in soon after retirement, suggested I carefully consider the consequences of my decision to quit work. "You've got to trust me on this one," I said. "I will never lack for things to do." I planned to celebrate by throwing out my alarm clock, which routinely went off at 4:00 a.m., and I made fantasy lists of ways to spend all that free time.

A week after I retired in early July, a meeting was scheduled for me with Dr. Bill Richards. In his email giving me directions to his office on the other side of the city from the research campus I'd visited, he wrote, "Though the amount of screening we're asking you to endure may feel excessive, please know that we want to ensure that possible participation in the project is really a wise decision for your personal/ spiritual growth and well-being." I appreciated the concern and was impressed by their thoroughness.

After a last-minute wrong turn, I arrived at Dr. Richards' office just on time. This genial man in his sixties quickly put me at ease, and we talked for an hour and a half in a comfortable office lined with books.

I was prepared to describe the sincerity and duration of my spiritual quest, but I wondered if my reading and introspection would be enough to qualify me for the program or if I'd need to demonstrate commitment to a religious practice. During our meeting I traced the evolution of my philosophy, and even described a few dreams I'd found significant. In one of my favorites, I found myself walking across thin air when boards in a pier were missing. When someone in the dream asked how I was able to do that, I answered confidently, "You must believe you are completely supported, even when there is no visible evidence." I woke up amazed. "Wow! I never could have thought of that on my own!" Since then I have returned to that advice many times. Dr. Richards seemed to like it too. His definition of spirituality appeared to be broad and inclusive, and my beliefs were never challenged.

I also took the opportunity to talk with Dr. Richards about the prerecorded soundtrack that I'd been told would accompany the all-day sessions, since he said he was "the music man" who had principally made the selections. I explained that music had a particularly strong hold on me. Because my attention always went directly to it, there was no such thing as "background music" in my world. My brothers and sisters used to claim that my middle name was "Turn-that-thing-down!" I have never been able to read, study, or do office work with music playing, and I couldn't imagine routinely plugging a device into my ear. Sometimes I leave a retail store (especially the bookstore, where I'm trying to concentrate) if I find the music there too intrusive. Even during a five-day drive across the country alone, I didn't once play the radio or a tape while on the road. Respecting its influence, I can carefully choose music to deepen or change my mood. My music library usually functions more like a medicine chest than an entertainment center.

Since I knew I would be confined with the music for the entire day of a session, I was concerned that it might overwhelm or sabotage the experience. Dr. Richards said that the soundtrack was primarily classical, which I prefer though I have not had a wide exposure to it. I would be required to listen to the same recording as all the other volunteers in order to maintain the consistency of the setting; the volume could be controlled through the headphones. He assured me that if I liked some of the pieces we had discussed during the interview, I would have no trouble with the selections.

Dr. Richards acted as the clinical supervisor for the States of Consciousness studies. He had been a primary guide for all 36 participants in the first study and for several in this second study. I enjoyed our visit and was sorry I would not be seeing him regularly.

After our talk I got out my map and drove across town to the Bayview campus again to continue the questionnaires for Mary. This time I was seated at her computer to answer a few hundred more items. I really didn't mind the exhaustive process. It was fascinating to be behind the scenes at such a groundbreaking research project.

Results of the First Study

Within two weeks of my meeting with Dr. Richards, the results of the first psilocybin study were released. Mary had alerted me that this would probably generate some publicity, but still I was surprised to see an article in the front section of *The Washington Post*[1] confirming what I'd already learned. Then I checked the institution's website for more details in the official press release.

Seeking new insights into brain function, I read, researchers had undertaken one of the first randomized, controlled studies on this substance since the events of the 1960s had relegated such drugs to "Schedule I" — illegal (with no sanctioned medical applications). Psilocybin was administered to 36 healthy, well-educated, middle-aged adults chosen from 135 applicants with active spiritual practices. Dr. Griffiths, the project's principal investigator, explained, "We thought a familiarity with spiritual practice would give them a framework for interpreting their experiences and that they'd be less likely to be confused or troubled by them."

In a first double-blind session, the 36 volunteers were randomly assigned to receive either psilocybin or methylphenidate (the stimulant known as Ritalin), 15 receiving psilocybin and 21 receiving Ritalin. In a second session two months later, those who had initially received psilocybin received Ritalin, 15 of those who had received Ritalin received psilocybin, and 6 volunteers received Ritalin for a second time. After the blind was broken, the 6 persons who had received two sessions with

Ritalin were offered a third unblinded session in which psilo-cybin was finally administered. More than 60% of the volun-teers reported effects that qualified as a "complete mystical experience" after taking psilocybin, and a third of those said it was the single most spiritually significant experience of their lifetimes. One-third of the subjects reported "strong or ex-treme" fear some time after taking psilocybin, though for many the fearful time was brief and transient.

The study, conducted over the course of five years, was praised for its rigorous protocol and hailed in the press release as a "landmark" approach to learning how certain hallucino-gens affect consciousness and sensory perception. Dr. Griffiths was further quoted as saying, "Establishing the basic science here is necessary to take advantage of the possible benefits psilocybin can bring to our understanding of how thought, emotion, and ultimately behavior are grounded in biology." Psilocybin had not been observed to be addictive or physically toxic in animal studies or human populations. [Appendix I]

This added more detail to the general information Mary had given me. I felt privileged to be considered for the second study, where volunteers were already receiving doses of varying strength that would provide a wide range of experiences.

But First, a Vacation

For someone with a generally quiet lifestyle, I was having an eventful year. My acceptance into the research program was not yet confirmed, but my trip to England was still on track. I had been inspired by Sir George Trevelyan who, in a book I'd read decades earlier, encouraged readers to make a pilgrimage to the ancient sacred sites in a spirit of reverence. I'd met this elderly gentleman on one of his visits to the U.S. in the 1970s, and was impressed with his warmth and bright energy.

I was able to find a tour group easily with an online search for the places I wanted to visit. The company's Arthurian tour had been cancelled that summer, so I signed up for their crop circle tour in July that included the three sites on my list. When I arrived at Heathrow I was greeted by guides Glenn and his wife Cameron, and joined the other members of the group from the U.S. and Australia. For nine days we were in the best of hands as we explored the beautiful countryside of southern England, principally in Wiltshire.

The morning after our arrival we visited a crop circle that had been minted just the night before. We trekked to three more that week, and met local experts who discussed some of the lore and theories of crop circle origins. Like others in the group, I examined how the wheat stalks were bent and admired the precise center whorls. We depended on aerial views posted on the Internet to see the overall patterns too intricate to be discerned from ground level.

The tour often followed the Michael and Mary ley lines, magnetic currents known since ancient times that run a diagonal path in Southern England. We danced on Silbury Hill and nosed into a prehistoric burial site where Glenn and a physicist in our group discussed the builders' careful juxtaposition of quartz rocks and limestone strata, which Glenn described as "electronics at the landscape level."

After visits to Avebury, Winchester and Wells, we spent a few days at Glastonbury, "the holiest soil in all England" according to legend, and at the end of the trip we had a special arrangement to visit Stonehenge at dawn. The tour was oriented toward phenomena rather than spirituality, but I was happy to be there all the same. I felt no need to account for the origins of the crop circles or to verify the energies of the ley lines. There was plenty of allowance in my philosophy for musing and mystery.

I enjoyed every day in the picture-book countryside of thatched-roofed cottages, lush gardens, fields and hedgerows, and with good company. I would have liked to stay all summer, but my budget was already strained. So by the end of the trip, when I could hardly lift my suitcase with all the new books I'd bought, I was content to be heading home. The visit to these historic areas and the heightened sense of discovery were a natural segue to the experiences that were to come at Johns Hopkins.

The Final Screening

About two weeks after returning from England, I drove to Baltimore for my final screening appointment for the study. I was apprehensive about meeting Dr. Roland Griffiths because I believed a failure to meet his approval could exclude me from the program, even after my previous examinations and interviews.

When Mary had walked me down the long corridor to his office I was greeted with a handshake by this man who fit the classic image of a professor in the Departments of Psychiatry and Neuroscience. Dr. Griffiths was tall and thin, with delicate glasses perched on his narrow face. His naturally fair coloring, close-cropped white hair, and his pale shirt and tie gave him a spectral appearance. I found him professional, reserved, and not a little inscrutable. His desk was piled high with neat stacks of reports and publications, and nearly every drawer in a formidable bank of file cabinets was labeled "Caffeine."

Consulting his paperwork, Dr. Griffiths began his own set of questions, particularly about my psychological and spiritual background. He asked about incidences of depression, use of alcohol, previous drug use, whether I still attended church after its prominent place in my personal history, if I were involved with spiritual groups of any kind, and about my current spiritual practices, especially meditation.

I told him that I had made a few attempts before, but was now trying again to learn to meditate, which I found a rather slippery exercise. I was reading about the methods, I said, but knew no one who meditated regularly and who could offer advice. I did not admit that I seemed to have a childishly short attention span whenever I tried it, that I was afraid I was doing it wrong, and was impatient when there seemed to be no results.

Dr. Griffiths thought it was unusual that I would undertake such an enterprise on my own. "Most people seem to find it's easier to learn when they participate in a group," he said, "which they may experience as producing a supportive 'field' or context." I replied that I knew of no such groups in my rural area, and that it seemed to me the responsibility still came down to individual effort. He agreed but thought that was nevertheless a more difficult route. I decided not to mention my concern of being distracted by the presence of others, at least while I was learning. There was something vaguely embarrassing about being in a group, I had found, and sometimes I was too self-conscious to concentrate. Any movement or sound would bring me out of my wobbly state.

"Many of our volunteers have a lot more experience at this," Dr. Griffiths commented. But he expressed interest in my notation of daily spiritual reading and asked, "Then you have regularly engaged in this practice as a sort of contemplative meditation?"

Of course I wanted his approval, and was grateful he was making some allowance to accommodate me. But regarded that way, my reading did honestly seem to qualify. "Well, yes," I said, "if you want to call it that. I thrive on reading spiritual books, and I can't bear to end the day without at least ten minutes with them to ground and reorient myself, no matter how long the day has been or how tired I am." He wrote a few comments on his yellow pad.

I was careful to provide succinct answers to Dr. Griffiths' questions to allow him to set the pace of the conversation. I was aware that he had measured many candidates against his strict criteria, and I was easily intimidated by his authority.

In response to his inquiries, I explained that I had made many adjustments in my philosophy over the years to attune to the highest truths that I had recognized. Even though I expected to continue my search for the rest of my life, I said, I had hopes that psilocybin could provide a glimpse of the Beatific Vision I sought, as a kind of "back door to the throne room."

Searching for an analogy, I offered, "It's like spending your whole life looking for the ocean, and then you have an opportunity to be lifted up to the top of a mountain where you can see that, ah yes, it *is* out there, sparkling in the sun, and you *are* going in the right direction. Even though you may not be able to maintain that perspective, at least you would be reinvigorated and reminded of the beauty and worthiness of your goal." Dr. Griffiths looked at me blankly as if this were so much misplaced romanticism, then very calmly stated that there was no guarantee I would have such an experience with psilocybin.

Those Pesky Risks

I was relieved when Dr. Griffiths appeared to be finished with the questions and turned his attention to the lengthy Consent Form, which I had signed on my previous visit. He provided me with a copy as well, and proceeded to read some paragraphs aloud as if they were new to us both. He concentrated on the sections emphasizing the risk factors, which made me uncomfortable because I didn't like to think that there *was* any reason to worry under their care.

> The primary effects of the hallucinogens, including psilocybin, are psychological. In larger doses, which you will receive in this study, psilocybin can bring about a very broad range of profound changes in perception and consciousness during the hours of drug action. There is a risk that you may find these effects unpleasant or frightening, though they are not always so…. You may experience anxiety, panic, or paranoia during the period of drug action. You may behave in ways such as intense crying, laughing, or panic that you might later find embarrassing. You may experience powerful emotions, both pleasant and unpleasant…. You may have dreams and/or enduring memories of drug session experiences. After a psilocybin session, there may be short-term to permanent changes in personality, attitude, or creativity.

The form went on to cover such possibilities as blood pressure increases, allergic reactions, stroke, heart attack, "or death" during psilocybin's activity, and short-term psychotic or anxiety disorders afterward. Even though I was assured that there was no harmful toxicity and virtually no chance of addiction, it was a relief to again notice the provision in the

Consent Form that I would be free to drop out of the study at any point.

Dr. Griffiths made it clear not only that I might not have a transcendental experience but also that I could confront all manner of unexpected psychological challenges, though he said it is often thought that these are the very issues most valuable for each of us to resolve. He added that on rare occasions volunteers had felt so suspicious of and threatened by their guides during a psilocybin session that they wouldn't even speak to them, only to realize the error when they were beginning to emerge from their altered state.

During this conversation, Dr. Griffiths several times used language I would not have expected in a scientific context. He was advising that I enter the experience "in all humility," truly open and willing to experience whatever might occur without setting conditions on it or trying to dictate its structure. He told me that I could confront "demons" in many guises, though they would be only projections of my own psyche. I understood his meaning, but it seemed incongruous to hear words such as "humility" and "demons" from this practical researcher.

He explained that although the risk of this substance pushing someone into schizophrenia could not be ruled out entirely, it seemed to have been overemphasized based on unregulated experiences of impressionable, possibly psychiatrically vulnerable subjects in the 1960s, some of whom had distinct genetic tendencies toward it. Dr. Griffiths said that he and his colleagues relied on careful screening to reduce that possibility, but I hadn't been aware of it to begin with.

In his role as the program's administrator, he had taken great care to review the possible consequences of my participation in the project. The other researchers also had emphasized the importance of taking the study seriously and being apprised of the risks. Each volunteer feels changed in some way, I had been told, although most seemed to believe it was for the better. By the time Dr. Griffiths had covered all these warnings, I felt that, despite all the trouble I had taken to qualify for the study, if I were turned down maybe that would be just as well after all.

As our talk concluded he said plainly, "I think you would be a good candidate for the program," as he checked his notes and tidied some papers. But he did not look at me while he spoke or offer a handshake and add, "And we would welcome your participation." He just walked me back down the hall.

After he left me in Mary's office, she told me that she and Matt would be my guides for the sessions. When I replied that I was not sure I had Dr. Griffiths' approval, she asked, "Didn't he tell you?"

I said, "Not in so many words," so I thought maybe there would be some further consultation or decision making.

I was pleased to be accepted for this second study, but after those caveats I also worried I might be inviting physical damage and acting irresponsibly toward the hard-won development of my lifetime. I remembered Matt's comment on my previous visit, "If you're fearful, that can be a good sign. It's an understandable reaction that shows you appreciate the risk. We'd be concerned if you *didn't* have any hesitation."

I liked to think I had established a solid foundation of self-knowledge and could handle some surprises, particularly if they were surfacing parts of my own psyche rather than external confrontations, but I was aware that areas of doubt and inadequacy remained. Besides, for all I knew psilocybin might

bypass the personality and tap directly into deeper, more unfamiliar levels where I could lose my way. I have some sense of
adventure, but I avoid dangerous situations. This seemed to
test the limits of my courage.

I told my sister I felt that I'd been chosen for the honor of
being thrown into a volcano. She laughed and said I should
instead imagine that I was training to be an astronaut and explore exotic new places. I'd reacted with the same happy excitement at first, then had to give due consideration to those pesky
risks. I was still considering whether to opt out, even before
figuring in the time, the cost of gasoline, and begging friends
to take me to Baltimore for the five sessions when I would not
be allowed to drive home. But then, was this not the rarest and
most exciting opportunity I could have ever imagined?

CHAPTER 2

Set and Setting

After my acceptance into the program, four two-hour meetings were scheduled for me to become better acquainted with Matt and Mary and get accustomed to the procedures for the psilocybin sessions. Because of my long drive, the staff was kind enough to schedule these in midday. Even to meet with them for that brief time meant the commitment of a full day for me.

These meetings were conducted in the actual session room that would become so familiar. It was located on the third floor where Matt, Mary, and Dr. Griffiths had their offices, but this was a windowless interior room accessed through a series of locked doors and circuitous passages, which added to its mystique. Though the room was attractively furnished, it was obviously of the same functional design as the other offices. One area was blocked off by tall partitions, which Matt moved as we entered to show that they concealed only ordinary desks and office equipment. It had not occurred to me to be suspicious about what might be behind them, but typically the staff was anticipating every question, every possibility.

Dominating the room was a contemporary white couch

with three black embroidered accent pillows, set off by a blue and red oriental rug. Two armchairs were available for the guides, and small tables with lamps gave the room a cozy, homelike atmosphere rather than relying on the overhead fixtures. My eye was drawn to several large paintings that brightened the walls and to a statue of the Buddha in an alcove. Across from the couch stood a bookshelf with an elaborate stereo, and the staff showed me the equipment for blood pressure readings under an end table. Two cameras and two pick-up microphones for videotaping were set unobtrusively in the ceiling. I also passed a desk near the room's entrance where volunteers filled out questionnaires after sessions.

It was a pleasant and comfortable setting, although I felt a little nervous to be confined in an area without a window. I told Mary I could understand that they would want to hold the sessions in an interior room which was isolated, but Mary said the reason was much more practical. The room was used because it was convenient and available.

During all our meetings there, my place was in the center of the couch, facing Mary in her chair, with Matt sitting in a chair to the side. Mary had been a guide with Dr. Richards for all 36 volunteers in the first study. I learned that Matt had helped draft the protocols and had worked with Mary and Dr. Richards as a guide for some of the other volunteers in this second study.

Mary and Matt always worked well together and complemented each other. In time I learned their specialties and their tastes, and which to address certain questions to. If I mentioned a tractor beam or the flux capacitor, Matt would know what I was talking about but Mary would look quizzical. If I cited Thomas Merton or Gryffindor, Mary would recognize the reference and Matt would be scratching his head. Between them, they had the territory covered — there was no doubt I was in good hands. When we started a meeting, Mary would ask that we close our eyes, and then she'd say a few words to deepen our focus and draw us into alignment.

Home, Work and Travel

Mary and Matt began the preparatory meetings by inviting me to tell them about myself. That would have seemed flattering if I hadn't known that the information was meant to provide some context for my reactions in an altered state. So I politely asked what they would consider a good starting point.

"How about your family, your relationship with your parents and siblings," Mary suggested.

As I'd stated on the questionnaires, my mother had died fourteen years earlier from alcoholism, and my father died two years after that from emphysema.

I am the oldest of eight children, born while my father was serving in WWII in the Pacific. My childhood was spent in an idyllic setting at my maternal grandparents' home beside a country church in Maryland. I happily played alone in a large yard and explored the barns, fields and cemetery, and received plenty of loving attention from my mother and grandmother. When my father returned from the war and more babies started arriving, he built a small house in scrub woods a mile away, where we moved when I was six. The gracious feeling of open space, security and leisure at my grandparents' gave way to cramped quarters and increasing family tension at the new house.

After me came three boys; I was nine years old when my first sister, Lisa, was born, and eleven at the arrival of my other sister, Alida. My mother's last child was born when I was twenty, which compounded her obligations and left me out of touch with my younger siblings. I also told Matt and Mary that the brother after me, who had been quite a hellion, died violently at age 30.

My father worked for 48 years as a mechanic and later a supervisor at the electric company in Washington, D.C. He seemed to have absorbed his mother's fatalism, "We're here to suffer." Family finances were always stretched thin. Nine of us shared two bedrooms separated by a half-wall where a lamp stayed on all night because mom was always getting up with a baby. When dad enlarged our house later, the bedrooms featured louvered doors "for heat circulation," which precluded any true privacy.

My mother and father did not appear to enjoy their children or display much affection toward them, and I felt deprived of good parental relationships. My dad, though intelligent and hard-working, was largely absent because of his obligations at work. My mother was emotionally troubled, and as an adolescent I seemed to catch the brunt of her increasing dissatisfaction with life. I was a good student, anxious to please at home and at school, but I couldn't seem to earn her approval. Although she liked to get me prettied-up for dances and proms, and my father always provided well for the family, I do not remember a single occasion when either of them put an arm around me or said "I love you." I learned it was easier to stay out of their way than to risk criticism or provoke an argument.

I attended twelve years of Catholic school, graduating at the top of a class of 36, and went on to a small college where my tuition and board were patched together with loans, grants, and scholarships. Remaining in the care of the nuns, I missed most of the social upheavals of the '60s. However, eventually I did capitalize on the sexual revolution. In my late twenties I lived for over a year with a man who had a young daughter. Later a man I call my ex (although I have never married) lived with me sometimes and traveled erratically for years. I would prefer to be in a relationship, but with time I have become increasingly clear about what conditions best promote my development and peace of mind, and often they have been met most appropriately by living alone.

I told Matt and Mary that I was non-competitive and had no career ambition. The level of job stress I was suited for was "shepherdess." My employment began in high school with part-time work on a weekly local newspaper, and continued in publishing after college. In 1990 I ended ten years of type-setting, editing and graphics freelancing in the Washington area when computer technology gave my clients comparable capacity in-house.

Soon after my mother died the following year, I sold, stored, or gave away most of what I owned and moved to Hawaii, which I had loved on a previous business visit, trying to finance the move on a shoestring. With this grandiose midlife gesture I looked forward to starting fresh and un-encumbered, living simply amid the beautiful setting of the islands. I'd done some research and thought I knew what to expect, but I had underestimated the difficulty of finding employment. When my resources ran out after a few months, even with temporary work, I gave up the venture and moved back to "the mainland."

Since I was already mobile and relatively unencumbered, I kept on exploring. I shipped my few household boxes to Reno, where my ex was living, and took a secretarial job. A year later I moved to Tucson alone for a position that I had arranged by phone from a magazine ad. I remained there about five years enjoying new friends and my work, which was not the job I had moved there for, although I never managed to adjust to the stark desert setting.

During this time, my father died after a slow decline and I returned home for his funeral. A few years later I packed up permanently and drove a rented truck towing my car back to the Washington area. Once our family's house was paid off, dad had finally become solvent, so each of the children had a small inheritance. Knowing how easily this sum could dissipate, I wanted to use it in a way that would make a difference in my life. My choice was a four-week trip to France and Italy with my former college roommate, perhaps my only opportunity for such travel.

When I returned, I stayed with my sister Lisa and her family for a few months, then found an administrative support position in the city suburbs. I rented an apartment while I looked for well over a year for a home with a little land to ensure my privacy and keep company with nature, but everything seemed too expensive. After expanding the search even farther afield, I signed the mortgage for a modest rambler with a large yard and several acres of woods. The property wasn't all I had hoped for and I didn't know the area, but it was affordable, and I was tired of looking.

My country setting came with another kind of price, though. I faced a two-hour commute every morning and again every evening, and longer when there were highway incidents. For seven years I seldom had a full night's sleep during the week, and everyone at the office knew I'd be napping during my lunch hour. I liked the job and the other employees, but all that driving had taken its toll. When I reached 62 and could retire, I said goodbye.

My Spiritual Evolution

From the moment I first read the ad for volunteers for the study, I was concerned about what the States of Consciousness researchers might consider valid spiritual qualifications. My interviews with Mary, Matt, Dr. Richards, and Dr. Griffiths had outlined my background on this topic, but in the four pre-paratory meetings I could fill in more details.

Our family was Roman Catholic, like most in our area. I was always devout, and never thought to question the doctrine presented to me. When we students were told the Catholic Church was the "one true Church," I could hardly believe my good fortune to have been born into it.

I remember assuring our parish priest that my religion was the most important thing in the world to me, and I meant it. The basic theology I absorbed, though cluttered with endless proscriptions, gave me a valuable introduction to abstract thought and a familiarity with the concept of higher powers, eternal life, divine providence, and a sense of larger community with believers in other places and times.

As a youngster the vague goal of "attaining salvation" was not nearly so appealing as the incidental trappings of the Church — the ceremonies, the rote catechism, rosary beads, patron saints, and the gilt-edged holy cards. I saved my money for the missions, I followed the Latin Mass in a thick missal which I had requested from my parents when I was 12, and for a time I played the organ for services.

I was in my teens when I first remember my father

speaking about his mother's experiences as a trance medium. We frequently visited Grandmother Estevez on Sundays, but I hadn't known she had such an exotic ability, and I was a little bashful to ask about it. She had discovered this as a girl in Cuba (though she and grandpapa were born in Spain) and at one time it had played a large part in her life. My father described lines of people outside their home waiting for a reading.

Grandmother told me about a book in Spanish in which the spirits themselves dictated their descriptions of life "on the other side of the veil" through human channels. It was fascinating to think that there was a source of knowledge about such things besides the formal doctrine of the Church. I resolved to find that book someday and have it translated so I could learn more.

For twelve years I was a conscientious student at our parochial school, compliant and respectful even when I chafed at the strict regimentation. But when I wanted to send applications to several non-Catholic colleges, the nuns and our parish priest refused to sign. Even my parents were afraid to confront them, so I was railroaded into four more years of Catholic education. With my conservative background I really was not prepared for much worldly exposure, which made the shelter of a small girls' school a blessing in disguise.

It was exciting to escape my rural roots at last and head for college in the suburbs of New York City. The liberal arts curriculum included four years of theology in addition to the academic courses and my major in fine arts. In particular I remember a third-year assignment to read dense, pedantic chapters from nine volumes on the Holy Spirit, incredulous that anyone could presume to write that much about something so obscure and unknowable. However, that same year

I was proud that I did not miss Mass and communion a single day.

I was dating a young man from Fordham University whose intellect and independence I greatly admired. Having reasoned his way out of a similar Catholic background, he knew how to bait me into arguments beyond the scope of standard dogma.

"Do you believe God is everywhere?" he asked.

"Of course. God is everywhere."

"Then how can He be more in the Eucharist than anywhere else?"

I would wail, "It's a mystery! The Church says it's a mystery!" Then I'd go back to my dorm, upset but intrigued, and say a rosary for his soul. When I saw him the next weekend I'd ask, "How'd that go again?" With patience, and no doubt great amusement, he needled me until I was forced to question much of my religious foundation. For the first time I was facing a serious challenge to my faith, and it was heady to realize I could think for myself.

I had always dutifully accepted the authority of my parents, the dictates of the Church, and the word of the nuns who were my teachers. I had limped through twenty years without having developed any skills at critical thinking or decision making. Until college, even my clothes were picked out for me. The school uniform was a shapeless navy blue jumper and white blouse, and for any other occasion I just asked, "Mama, what do I wear?" I had learned the unhappy consequences of *not* getting this approval.

My boyfriend had argued that in order to choose between two paths, such as the dictates of religion and the empiricism of science, one must weigh the merits of each with detachment. He chided that I could not be impartial because I was a dyed-in-the-wool theist unable to imagine any alternative to the existence of God, and he was disappointed that I did not prefer reason and logic as he did. He was correct about me — doubt was impossible — and our philosophies could not be reconciled.

I may not have changed enough to suit him, but I had to admit that my perspective had already shifted irrevocably. If I was assuming authority for what I believed, what was the role of the Church?

One cold Sunday morning in my senior year I quietly got ready for Mass as usual. I told my roommate to go ahead without me and maybe I'd join her later. I hesitated briefly, then put on my coat and left the dorm.

It took all my courage to turn away from the chapel and walk around the block. For a while I sat on a stump, looking at my watch and thinking, "By now they're up to the Offertory. If I miss that, I'm essentially missing Mass. How do I feel? Should I run over to chapel?" A little time went by. "Now they're up to the Consecration …" And still I sat there, deliberately stepping outside the familiar, trying to sort out my reactions and see whether this would force the issue with my conscience. Though many people consider themselves "fallen-away Catholics," that was not the case with me. I made a hesitant but life-altering decision that winter day, and I remember it well. It was neither laziness nor defiance, but a simple, tentative, difficult, and lonely step of separation.

The last stronghold of my faith was the Eucharist, the belief that the priest's blessing could transform a wafer of bread into the Body of Christ. Even after I questioned this, I often went to Communion with everyone else at family weddings and funerals just in case Christ really was present in that sacrament in a special way. Until I could be sure it wasn't true, I felt I should take advantage of the opportunity, besides allaying my family's suspicions about my devotion. But when the issue went on without any resolution, I put it on the shelf, hoping time would sort it out.

The delicate matter of distinguishing religion from theology took many more years as I learned to extend beyond the Church's structure and teachings. I was not attending services during that time, nor did I consider myself a Catholic, but I still had an affection for the imagery and rituals, with the exception of the groveling language of the prayers. In that "consciousness-raising" era of civil rights and women's liberation, I became aware that we were addressing God as some implacable despot, and the Virgin Mary and saints as fawning intercessors. *"To thee do we cry, poor banished children of Eve. To thee do we send up our sighs, mourning and weeping in this valley of tears. Turn then, most gracious advocate, thine eyes of mercy toward us, and after this our exile show unto us the blessed fruit of thy womb, Jesus."*

Instead of the poetry I once saw in those prayers, they had come to sound antiquated and overwrought. If we are really children of God, made in His image and likeness, why would we be such miserable supplicants? By then I had my own apartment, a good job, and casual friends, but there was no one in my life with a similar interest in spirituality who could discuss these things with me.

I was in no hurry to replace one system of belief with another, and it was several years before I became involved with another group. A new acquaintance introduced me to the teachings of Paramahansa Yogananda, my first exposure to

Eastern traditions. She urged me to read his autobiography and sign up for his organization's lessons by mail, and I began to attend her group's Sunday meditations in Washington. Now I was supposed to learn new prayers and ceremonies and a different pantheon of holy faces. Soon my friend pressed me to join their study group as well.

"So what's that like?" I asked. "Do you read from Yogananda's book and then talk about the teachings?"

She immediately corrected me. "Oh no, we never discuss anything. That would be interpretation, and that can come only from Mother Center in California."

I recognized a familiar ring ... hmmm, kind of like "infallibility." Even though I studied the lessons for a year, I could not bring myself to take the initiation that would pledge me to their guru not just for this lifetime (as I understood it) but for all eternity. That was my last encounter with organized religion.

Another turning point came when my father gave me a book by a popular psychic. Dad had always set an example as an obedient, observant Catholic, but he was clearly commending the book's message of reincarnation. He was acquainted with this from his mother's trance experiences, yet the concept was squarely outside the Church's teaching. I then found myself challenged to accept the possibility of reincarnation, and with it, the implication that my religious background was not comprehensive enough. If this were true, what else might I need to question, discard, or adopt? With careful consideration, I concluded that the notion of reincarnation solved more problems than it created, and I inched farther out on the limb.

After reading a few similar books, I became acquainted with the writings of Edgar Cayce, and made several trips to attend seminars and lectures at the organization he founded in Virginia Beach. This body of work had limited interest for me, but it was there that I first learned of the Findhorn Community in Scotland and heard talks by co-directors Peter Caddy and David Spangler, who impressed me with their fresh ideas and penetrating spirituality. The wider circle of this community included Sir George Trevelyan, whose writings prompted my eventual trip to England.

Much new channeled material was becoming available at that time — the modern equivalent of my grandmother's book in Spanish I had hoped to find. My favorite was Seth, written through Jane Roberts. His approach was cold and brilliant, and the detailed information he offered on the structure of the universe was (and remains) unparalleled. In the 1980s I was drawn to the spiritual tone of Bartholomew, channeled by Mary-Margaret Moore. When I left for Hawaii, four of his books were in my suitcase. Now all five sit on my coffee table, and I am still finding new depths in passages I marked years ago. The phrase I carry closest to my heart is Bartholomew's exhortation, "Ask to expand." [2]

Later I became acquainted with the writings of another influential teacher who has remained a staple in my spiritual life, Joel Goldsmith. This ordinary American had found his way by trial and error, following his heart as I had, and reached a deep level of revelation.

I attended some Sufi meditations at one time but had not delved into Buddhism or other religions of the East since I was already strongly grounded in Christianity. However, after the many references during the Johns Hopkins program, I became more curious about these. Even in rereading Bartholomew's work, which was always expressed in broad, universal terms beyond any religious system, I suddenly realized that his orientation sounded distinctly Eastern.

I experimented with a few psychic readings, a past-life regression, a Native-American soul retrieval, and a shamanic workshop, but I always returned to my beloved books as my best teachers and companions.

When I investigated other schools of thought, I weighed each carefully over a long period of time, often years, to determine whether it fit in with my working model or if the new idea required that my beliefs be adjusted. I would keep it in mind as I regarded the routine aspects of my life. "Does this explain things more clearly? If I knew this to be true, would I act differently?"

Because of my experience with Catholicism, I had become wary of teachings that seemed rigid or authoritarian. How can you get credit for believing or practicing something, I wondered, unless you consciously choose it for yourself? If you just accept blindly what you are told, how can that strengthen your capacity for discovery and discernment or ever allow you to make personal progress? I had been appalled to hear one well-known fundamentalist preacher on TV promoting cassette tapes which, he assured, would tell you "what you believe and why you believe it."

Over many years I had learned the value of trusting my intuition instead of the obedience that my parents and teachers had always promoted as such a virtue. I had also found that intuition partnered nicely with reason and common sense. With these criteria I could fearlessly examine any fact or theory and assess how accurate it sounded. Developing this ability is truly an art in itself, demanding constant inquiry, honesty, receptivity, and persistence.

As I had tried to fashion a living, practical philosophy, I was encouraged to find inspiring new sources becoming more widely available. The call that drew me forward over the years in fits and starts is exactly the guidance that directed me to the States of Consciousness study — of that I have no doubt. I told Mary and Matt that I felt that I had a compact with the Divine even before I entered this life: just give me a fair chance, and I will find my way back home.

I shared these personal narratives with the staff during the preparatory meetings, with other diversions and opinions. Occasionally, we would lob around a premise to compare our viewpoints. At one point Mary said, "Are you aware how often you're quoting someone else?" Yes, I was. I explained that it was partly because the material had already been expressed better than I could say it. Then too, I was accepting someone else's word for an experience or conclusion that I had not reached on my own.

I did not feel qualified to declare, for example, that every thought creates worlds and that every option is actualized in some alternate reality, even though I was inclined to accept it. Instead I'd just acknowledge that as Seth's.[3] If anyone wanted to dispute it or check the source for themselves, they might be more disposed to believe words in print or attributed to an outside authority.

I have adopted the phrase "It is my understanding that ..." to preface concepts I have not confirmed but that I choose to use as working models. My conversation may have come across as hesitant and unoriginal, but I felt it was better to be honest about my level of advancement rather than pretending I knew all this from experience. However, Mary clarified that she hadn't meant to confront me, only to invite me to speak from my own authority about these subjects as I had come to know them.

Learning to Trust

Besides an outline of how I arrived at this point in my life, Mary said I would be asked to share my most personal issues with her and Matt in order to foster our trust and rapport. Describing my background and my strengths was one thing, but exposing my vulnerabilities to these new acquaintances made me a little uncomfortable.

A scheduled meeting with employees in a professional office building with locked doors, security guards, and cameras did not seem conducive to developing trust on demand. I would have favored a more equalizing and informal setting, like all of us going out for coffee, but I could see that was not about to happen. Owning up to my most troublesome areas seemed to put me at a social disadvantage. Were Matt and Mary going to confide *their* weaknesses to *me*? Not likely. Were they going to look at each other after I left and say, "The poor thing really has problems, doesn't she?" Entirely possible. And yet my assignment remained: tell us about yourself, and your deepest secrets.

In all fairness, it was neither difficult nor threatening to share my "secrets" with my guides, since I am not haunted by any major offenses or regrets. When I finally worked up to confessing the worst of my concerns, Mary said, "But Maria, *everyone* has fears and feelings of shortcomings." Well, okay then, maybe that's not so bad. Thanks.

Mary and Matt never appeared to be judgmental or critical, and I felt no need to conceal delicate matters. I suspected that any random contents of my mind might come tumbling out while in an altered state, and knew they needed a context for it in case I required help. I was weaving my own safety net as I talked.

Instead of the prospect of being wafted up to blissful communion with the Divine during these explorations, the staff's coaching centered on the worst-case scenarios. Matt informed me, "Psilocybin contains no images, no feelings. It's only a chemical, and current theory is that all it does is open up the barriers that keep us in our everyday thought patterns. Whatever you perceive is the product of your own mind, so you control your reaction to it. The only thing you can possibly meet in an altered state is *you*."

Mary told me that some volunteers appreciated the opportunity to deal with their shadows, telling the staff that their psychological struggles during those sessions were as effective as a year of therapy. But I still thought that there must be easier ways to resolve such problems than a cage match with them during the activity of a mind-altering substance. This suggested that each of us has a dark subconscious strewn with potential landmines.

After all this advice, I became fairly convinced that the hallucinogen would show me a personification of my fears. The media have given us many memorable special-effects creatures, but I knew that this bogeyman would be custom-designed for (and by) me. I was not so sure I'd be able to deal with such a demon if my state of mind were distorted, no matter how much preparation I'd made. Perhaps I would be ambushed by vulnerabilities even I wasn't aware of.

The staff emphasized that I should enter the experience with psilocybin "in complete humility" — that word again — without expectation, and be willing to go wherever it led, whether to terror or transcendence. "Humility" always seemed an unlikely term, suggesting a contrived or even forced submission, or maybe for me it was still freighted with years of Catholic indoctrination. The staff used it to mean an attitude of openness rather than an admission that you had no power and were not allowed to think for yourself.

I was curious and willing to make new discoveries, but saw no way to avoid judging these from my established perspective. Would that invalidate the experience for my development or the purposes of the research? If I failed to be open would I misinterpret what I found? Would the staff be able to tell whether I was getting it wrong? I would soon learn that they could indeed.

Dr. Griffiths instructed me to completely release any preconceptions about what might happen during the activity of psilocybin. He advised me to exist only in that moment in time, without baggage or expectations, willing to accept any experience without judgment. I was to merely observe the unfolding scenes passively: "Go where it takes you." I should not, he said, under any circumstances give in to fear or allow myself to be sidetracked with personal matters. If something confronted me, I was just to make a note of it and let it be. "If you run from it," Dr. Griffiths warned, "I can guarantee you will spend hours in misery."

I nodded because I understood the instructions, not because I had any confidence that I could carry them out. I tried to rehearse in my imagination that I would stay open and alert, trusting that the journey would end up more or less where it began, back in the same the room with the staff.

In one of our meetings after a preparatory session with Matt and Mary, Dr. Griffiths compared the altered perceptions of the psilocybin experience to the states of consciousness one encounters after death. He explained that the Tibetans would gather around the deceased person to read and chant from the Book of the Dead to remind the lingering soul of the eternal truths, and that he need not be afraid of this next phase in which he found himself. Dr. Griffiths quoted to me, "Remember who you are, child of noble birth." I loved those words, and they went straight to my heart like an arrow. Now if we could only keep that in mind while we go about our business *before* death, I thought.

On another occasion, Dr. Griffiths gravely counseled that when I encountered the high dose of psilocybin I could feel I had been overdosed. I might think that I should have told them I was "crazier than I had let on," he said, and that now it was too late and I was being pushed past the brink of sanity. He told me I would be able to handle the experience and that I would be recognizably myself when I surfaced again.

Oh, great. This was sounding more ominous all the time. I begged Mary and Matt for assurance that none of the volunteers had emerged with permanently mangled identities, and that I'd come through it all right. Yes, yes, of course, they said. Then why was I being given such dire warnings? Should I back out before I even started? I felt like I was being stuffed into a cannon and the fuse was being lit.

The Final Countdown

Even with careful preparation and personal attention from these experts in the field, I knew there was no way to anticipate what I might encounter during the session, nor could the staff give me any guarantees. I was eager to get further information on the process.

Among the small array of books in Mary's office, one in particular caught my attention: *Cleansing the Doors of Perception* by Huston Smith. Like the Huxley essay, the title referenced a quotation from poet and mystic William Blake, "If the doors of perception were cleansed, everything would appear as it is, infinite." [4] I ordered a copy of the book to find out more about altered states.

I had not known Smith's name and work, but I learned he was well known as a scholar of comparative religion and that he holds a unique place in the modern study of entheogens. He was on the scene in the 1960s as an associate of Timothy Leary and Aldous Huxley, and he provided his own accounts of mind-altering hallucinogenic experiences. Though Smith claimed that his encounters with mescaline and psilocybin were among the most important of his life, after intense experiences he stated plainly, "I am afraid of the entheogens," and said that in retrospect he had no desire to take them again. [5] Despite his familiarity with these substances, Smith maintained a healthy respect: sacramentally, not recreationally.

The discussions and counseling were helping me feel more at ease with the staff and the setting at Johns Hopkins. But one afternoon as Mary, Matt and I were ending a routine meeting, I regained my perspective about how one-sided this exchange really was. When I casually asked Matt if he had any plans for the upcoming Labor Day weekend, he said, "I'm going to be in a wedding." I didn't know whether it would be polite or intrusive to inquire further, but I was really surprised when he added it was *his* wedding! The focus had always been on my life, my issues, so I was embarrassed not to be aware that something so important was going on in his. I offered my congratulations.

As the countdown to the first psilocybin session continued, Matt and Mary began to introduce me to the format of the sessions themselves.

Mary explained that the white couch would be outfitted with flannel sheets over a waterproof pad, in the unlikely event of loss of bladder or bowel control. (I remembered that was mentioned in the Consent Form, but it didn't increase my confidence.) A bathroom was just down the hall. A pan was tucked away discreetly in case I should vomit, though this was not expected. My blood pressure would be monitored regularly, more frequently when it might rise during the height of the effects, and the cuff would remain on my arm for most of the session. Two video cameras would record the entire session, but, Mary said, the tapes were just routinely archived.

The staff would provide a red rose and a bowl of fresh grapes for each session, and I would be invited to examine the rose at break intervals, which I presumed would indicate any hallucinations. They instructed me to bring a light lunch, such as a sandwich or fruit, and also said I could place mementos or photographs in the room if I wished.

"Can I talk during the session?" I asked. "Is that a stupid question? Will I even be capable of talking? Do other volunteers talk or are we supposed to be quiet and concentrate?" Mary said some volunteers talked a great deal and others very little. It would be up to me.

After our discussions, Mary and Matt removed the cushions from the back of the couch so I could recline and become accustomed to the procedures. They placed the headphones over my ears and began the soundtrack. "High-class system," I said. "I wish I had something this good at home."

The music began with a melodic guitar concerto that I

inquired about. Vivaldi, Mary told me. We were all quiet for a
time while the recording played both in my headphones and
into the room from the speakers. It was comfortable there, and
I felt safe with the two of them. Free to relax into the setting, I
could allow myself to be swept away, and found a poignant
emotion in one of the ending chords. "Listen to that!"

I asked whether I should leave the headphones in place or
if they were optional, and was told that they were considered
part of the protocol. The musical selections had been carefully
chosen to begin subtly, to evolve in character as the volunteer
responded to the action of the entheogen, and then to transition back toward the original setting at the end of the session.
The two guides would also hear the music directly from the
stereo.

We tried the arrangement again at the end of the next
preparation meeting, adding the light-blocking eye mask. The
world was being shut out in stages as I rehearsed for the inward journey. I had no idea what pieces would be played as the
day went on, but I expected they would largely determine the
cast of my experience. I was not sure I had ever convinced the
staff that I had a peculiar sensitivity to music, and wondered if
that were just some claim to elitism.

When Mary was taking me downstairs to sign out after
one of these meetings, I commented on her job. "You screen
18 volunteers and explain the procedures to them, and then
you have to sit with them all day for five sessions each, listening to the same soundtrack over and over? That must get
pretty boring." Mary replied that it was anything *but* boring,
and she added enthusiastically, "I love my job!"

As we completed our final preparations, I told Matt and
Mary a dream I remembered from my college years. I was

sitting with an angel up in a large tree by the church beside my childhood home. The angel offered to take me far out into the universe to places I had never seen. I was afraid he might mean taking drugs like LSD, which were believed to permanently alter or damage DNA, a concern that Matt said had later been shown to be scientifically unfounded. I wanted to go with the angel, but I worried that we might never find our way back, so I declined.

Mary asked, "And what would you say now?"

I smiled mischievously. "I'm sitting here on your couch, aren't I?"

Did I really have to wait this long to explore other realms? I probably could have clicked my ruby slippers together at any time, but like most people, I didn't realize it. The distraction of "the ten thousand things" and the need to earn a living had cost a delay of decades. But now, beginning another phase of my life, I could direct my attention elsewhere and enjoy the luxury of more leisure and choice.

I had first read about the psilocybin study in January and I had finished the tests and met most of the researchers before I left work six months later. Once I had returned from my trip to England and received final approval, I was ready to actively begin the program.

At first I had viewed my participation as a diversion from daily routine and an interruption of whatever practical path I would find after retirement. But some well-placed comments from Matt and Mary began to persuade me that this was not a temporary jog or an angle in the path so much as a new door that had suddenly opened in front of me, a natural progression of my spiritual development.

The fourth and last of my preparatory meetings was

completed in mid-September, exactly a week before my first psilocybin session was scheduled. Everything was in order. I had lost the last few pounds, I had gathered my courage to proceed, and I had done some homework to prepare. We could begin.

CHAPTER 3

What Have I Done?

My first session with psilocybin was scheduled for a Wednesday in mid-September. All of my preparations with the research team — the medical exam, the lengthy interviews, the questionnaires, and the four initial meetings with the staff — plus all my readings and reflections over nine months had built up to this day.

I reviewed the list of procedures. I was instructed to keep my schedule light the days before and after the session. I could not take unapproved medications or herbs during the week before the session because of possible interaction with the psilocybin, or drink alcohol 24 hours before or after the session. I was to eat a small, low- or non-fat breakfast that morning and bring a light lunch. I should arrive at 8:00 a.m. and wear comfortable clothing. I was not allowed to drive a car or operate heavy machinery for at least 12 hours afterward. And I was to write a report of the session before the meeting with my guides the next day.

I got up about 3:15 a.m. that morning, packed a travel bag, had a bite of breakfast, and got on the road before 5:00 a.m. An hour later I arrived at the home of my sister Alida, who had taken a day off from work to drive me to Baltimore. We chatted on the two-hour trip, and I had something else to eat to help sustain me through the morning hours, being careful to leave a required interval before the administration of the psilocybin. Alida dropped me off at the Behavioral Research building in time for my appointment and then set out for a day of shopping.

Toting an armload of gear, I signed in at the front desk and was escorted upstairs by a young assistant, Ben, to wait in Mary's office while the session room was being set up. As part of the protocol, I was sent to the ladies' room to provide a urine sample. The staff wanted to account for every contingency, including whether a volunteer had taken drugs *before* ingesting the psilocybin.

Since I'd been invited to bring along personal mementos, I assembled a few trinkets that would be visually appealing if I were having hallucinations. I brought some toiletries and a change of clothes "just in case," a pillow roll to place under my knees, and a light lunch, according to the instructions. I had put on my thick glasses instead of my hard contact lenses when I got up early that morning, then I decided there'd be no need for the lenses if I'd have an eye mask all day. And for that matter I could do without makeup, too.

The session format allowed for breaks when the volunteer could go to the bathroom, have lunch, and look around the room to offer comments about perceptions. I was interested to see how my surroundings might appear changed, remembering Huxley's reports.

I knew that psilocybin was the synthetic equivalent of "magic" mushrooms, and I could appreciate why the researchers would prefer to use the version of known purity that could be measured precisely. The psilocybin used in this study was synthesized at Purdue University, the staff told me, though the capsules were filled on-site at Johns Hopkins by a pharmacist who alone knew their dosage. None of the project staff knew in advance, not even Dr. Griffiths, and certainly not the volunteer.

I understood that I could receive a low, medium, medium-high, or high dose, or the placebo. However, I did not know at first that the medical lab and the pharmacy itself were located in the same building where the sessions were held. Not only was every dose strictly accounted for, but the psilocybin was kept under lock and key — "literally in a bank vault," Matt said. No one could conveniently shake a few capsules out of the bottle as they passed by.

While the room was being set up, Dr. Griffiths visited with me in Mary's office, not quite closing the door, to ask how I was feeling. I admitted that I had butterflies, but my curiosity was stronger than my anxiety. Dr. Griffiths advised me once again to be completely humble and to go willingly wherever the experience took me.

Walking down the hall to the session room, I felt like an astronaut being ushered out to the ship. Even though I'd been in that room for every preparatory meeting, there was an added drama that morning as passcards opened doors and we turned corners that led into farther rooms.

Everything was in place as I expected. There was a single red rosebud in a tall vase and a large blue glass bowl of grapes on a table, and the couch was made up with sheets and blanket. Mary and Matt stood alert and smiling, ready to guide me through the day. It all looked familiar, but now there was a new, keen sense of anticipation.

First I reclined on the couch, listening to the guitar concerto that opened the day's soundtrack while Matt took a baseline blood pressure reading, a routine procedure before every session. When that was complete, the last of the preparations was in place and the runway was clear.

I took a seat in the center of the white couch, and the three staff members drew up their chairs nearby. Mary presented me with a plastic box with slots for pills, but containing only one dark blue capsule, and invited me to confirm that the name on the box was mine. I tilted up my glasses to look more closely … and yes, it was. Mary carefully removed the capsule and set it into the shallows of a crudely shaped brown goblet that looked like handmade pottery. Matt told me it was an authentic vessel from the Central American region where the mushrooms are used in native rituals.

Mary, Matt, and Dr. Griffiths offered smiles, praise, and good wishes as they improvised a little ceremony. My role was to swallow the capsule and wash it down with a full glass of water as they instructed. After a few more kind words, Dr. Griffiths departed and I talked quietly with my guides as we waited for the substance to take effect, if in fact I had received an active dose, which Matt said would be about half an hour.

Into the Abyss

For this short block of time I had brought a binder of art clippings to show Mary and Matt the kind of imagery I wanted to incorporate into some paintings I had in mind. They sat beside me on the couch as I turned the pages and commented on the items.

In about twenty minutes I began to feel a strong physical reaction which could only be the effects of psilocybin, and I knew I had to get into position right away. I put down the binder, made a hurried trip to the bathroom with Mary following and waiting at the door, then reclined on the couch as Mary set the eye mask and headphones in place and put a blanket over me. Matt wrapped my arm with the cuff to check my blood pressure at intervals throughout the session.

All my senses seemed to be collapsing inward. There were sensations of falling, being weighted into unnatural heaviness and sinking into the unknown. I quickly began to lose touch with all that surrounded me — the people, the room, every useful reference — as I plunged into turmoil I was in no way prepared for. I mumbled a few words to Matt and Mary to let them know I was already becoming lost, and I tried to send back even the most elementary reports on what was happening to me. A spicy blast like chili pepper rampaged through my digestive track. Darkness closed in as I gave up control of both my body and my rational mind.

Matt told me later that as I was slipping into the abyss I was murmuring, "What have I done? What have I done?" With despair and regret, I realized there was no way to reverse the decision. I was gone.

Whatever I might have imagined a hallucinogenic experience to be like, this was not it. Becoming unmoored from everything I recognized was one thing, as I was shut into blackness, disoriented, and unable even to stand. But within moments even the organizing principle of self began to unravel. The simple security of waking consciousness gave way to a confusion like being drunk or trying to claw my way back from the chemical grasp of anesthesia. I was being bumped and rattled past the limits of sanity, and all I could do was hang on for dear life.

Then, adding to the mental stress, involuntary physical spasms set in as well. I felt spring-like contractions in my lower abdomen, up against my backbone, strong enough to send a jolt down my lower body and jerk my legs, and sometimes my left arm flailed sympathetically. These tremors came in irregular bursts and remained with me until the effects of the psilocybin played out later in the day. I was grateful that they were not also in my chest or I thought it was possible my heart would stop.

I could hear Mary and Matt talking to me calmly and in-forming me that sometimes volunteers did have these physical responses, but I hadn't been warned about any such thing. They reminded me that psilocybin was one of the safest hallu-cinogens available and that I would emerge all right. That was easy for them to say — they weren't drowning.

I had a vague sensation of moving through netting like cobwebs, but still it was black-on-black, more of a feeling than an image. There were a few fleeting indications of light or color, but hardly describable. The descent continued until I seemed to be violently shaken in a bottle of black ink.

Mary was encouraging me to flow through this without resistance, even if I didn't like what was happening. I heard her instructions clearly but was not able to comply. I found myself desperately clinging to my tenuous grip on my identity, maybe even existence itself. I did not feel like I was "in my right mind," and was far beyond decision making. It was difficult to focus at all. Surrendering to the beautiful and the Divine is one thing, but surrendering to misery and helplessness is some-thing else again. Surely that could not have been what they were asking.

I had never experienced anything like this. Although

distressed and distracted, I was still amazed to find myself involved in two realities at once. While being churned through frightening dimensions, I was also aware of lying on the couch where I could talk with Matt and Mary. I had no idea how both could be true, but this was not the time for armchair philosophy.

I would have begged them to rescue me except I knew it was impossible; the substance would have to run its course. I was being dragged under this tide and there was nothing to be done. The roiling blackness became punctuated by bursts of bright geometrics. These were not just circles or squares or squiggles, but flashes of complex figures in seemingly random patterns, appearing and disappearing with no discernible sequence or purpose.

The music in the headphones now was booming aggressively, driving me on at a frantic pace rather than providing any support or comfort. I knew that the carefully arranged music track was part of the protocol, but it felt like a terrible imposition, and I wished I were allowed to rip off the headset. I had enough to handle without being strong-armed into a particular reaction, and I wanted to yell, "Don't tell me what I'm supposed to be feeling!" If this was where the staff expected me to respond with awe, obviously I was not following the plan.

Mary had suggested beforehand that I should not divert my attention to wondering about the name of a piece of music, but during the experience I was too overwhelmed to care. I noticed a loud, strong choral work, and somewhere I caught the thread of a *Kyrie Eleison*, but that was about all. At another time, Mary read me some passages I had marked in a favorite book, but they too were useless, irrelevant, beyond comprehension. I was fighting for my life and someone was handing me a daisy.

One unfamiliar music selection browbeat me beyond mercy. I gasped that I could not understand why they would play such a frightening piece for anyone who was so defenseless, but Mary was still advising me not to be concerned. That was followed by an eerie and unsettling chorale that kept up the ominous tone.

I had been led to believe that I would either have a transcendental experience of communion with the Divine or I would confront psychological demons that I was supposed to acknowledge and dismiss, but neither was happening. There was only an unnamed, unseen enemy in the form of a relentless battering. I found myself a captive in some netherworld I had no way of anticipating or escaping.

As I struggled in this turbulence I couldn't find any direction or source of information. I would not have said I was fearful because there was no particular threat I could name, but certainly I was stressed to my limits and worried about the effects of those spasms racking my body. The sensation was like being swept along on a strong current in a river, plunged over rapids and slammed up against obstacles, out of control. I kept telling Matt and Mary I felt helpless as I moved further and further from anything that could anchor me in known reality.

Several times my awareness of self fell off a ledge and consciousness was lost completely, an altered state within an altered state. I have no idea where I went, but occasionally I would find myself returning from it to the physical shaking and the sinking blackness. Once or twice I thought maybe I was going to die, and was sorry I didn't feel better prepared for it.

But I suspected that I might not be released so easily, and instead would have to work through the full range and power of this substance that had taken ownership of me.

I was hoping that after I passed through certain stages the landscape would lighten and I could ease into some respite of calm or peace, but as the assault continued I began to doubt whether any breakthrough or revelation could be worth the terrible price. I would surface enough to recognize my surroundings, then sink again into the chaos.

Oddly enough, throughout this experience I remained alert to social manners — maybe not what one would expect under duress, but an indication that the personality still maintained its judgments. Even though my guides were doing their best to accommodate me, I wanted to complain. A couple of times I was distracted by Matt's commentary and wanted to request quiet, and also I wanted to ask Mary to move away and stop holding on to me, but I did neither because I knew their intentions were kind and I did not want to criticize or insult them. My sorry condition was no excuse to be rude. However, I did finally speak up about the music. They couldn't get the psilocybin out of my system, but Matt and Mary *did* have control over that stereo. Having reached my limits, I found the courage to ask if they could turn it off.

I knew the ordeal would eventually play itself out even if there was nothing identifiable to confront, but in time I became so unfocused that I could not speak at all, drifting in and out of waking consciousness. As I tossed fitfully, I ran my hand up across my forehead and through my hair again and again, and tried to suppress anxious little noises. The abdominal shudders were still causing my legs to jerk. My whole world was shaking to pieces, and I just wanted to survive.

After one of those mysterious side trips I found myself on the white couch again in complete quiet — no music, no talking, just blessed silence. I was relieved and grateful, though the spasms were as strong as ever. The eye mask was still in place, so my world remained dark. After several hours, I had probably passed the farthest extreme of the experience. As it leveled off, the situation began to improve, ever so slowly.

Only after this point did anything distinctive appear beyond impressions and reactions. My attention was drawn to the activities at my body's cellular level. I seemed to be intruding on a very private world there which operated with its own logic and rhythm, as if I had stumbled onto the secrets of some alien race, or turned over a rock that harbored a colony of strange bugs. The cells understood that I was watching, and so much as asked, "What are *you* doing here? What do *you* want with us?" They showed no antagonism, just surprise. I became aware that they were following directives much like emotions, always working efficiently without question or error, and certainly without interference from my conscious mind. I backed off and left the cells to their business, amazed to have come upon that odd quarter at all.

Toward the end of the deepest gulf of separation, I briefly glimpsed some small point of pale light that appeared as distant from me as the earth is from the center of the galaxy. This was offered as a gift of peace, a gesture of kindness, as the rough waters began to subside.

A few practical matters began to spring up like buoys as I edged toward shore again. I remembered that I was supposed to spend the night at my sister's, and that I had planned to run errands the next day. I dismissed these thoughts because I was still too occupied with staying afloat to be concerned about whatever dimension errands were in. I also wondered what time it was, but didn't bother to ask because it would have required too much effort to make sense of the answer.

Sometimes I spoke to Mary and Matt, but there was little to describe until I gradually returned to the reality of the couch. I longed to feel the sensations of the earth again, and babbled that I wanted to be at home, in my yard, in fresh air. I thought that if I could just find my way back to the physical world and if someone would take me outside, I would run off like a wild animal and would never, ever go into a building again. I needed a retreat with total simplicity where I could hide away and regain my strength.

I was exhausted by the shaking, and my abdomen ached as if I'd been doing exercises for hours. Every cell called for a bath in cold, fresh water. There were other immediate and demanding sensations as well. I remember saying, "It's not pain, but it's like pain," though later I could not reconstruct what I'd been experiencing.

Mary suggested to Matt that they help me sit up to take a drink of water. I was thirsty, but not sure at all that my body could manage to get up, as unnaturally heavy as it still felt. But once they had raised my shoulders so I could drink from a glass, the new position assured me that I could establish some control and inhabit my ordinary world once more.

Finding My Way Back

As I began to surface again, rational thinking made a tentative return. I found words — my friendly, familiar words — tucked among the crevices of gray matter where I'd lost track of them. Sentence structures reappeared from the thickets. As the connection strengthened, words came pouring out in a torrent, and I began to talk incessantly. Language was the lifeline by which I reeled myself back to the world I knew.

I tried to give Matt and Mary a report on the unaccustomed territories, both for their records and so they could tell me later what sort of nonsense had come out of my mouth, because my impressions faded quickly and my thoughts had little continuity.

By then I was sitting up, my eyes closed and the spasms less vigorous. Mary was right beside me on the couch, and I felt constricted. Not wanting to complain, I struggled for some diplomatic way to make a request: "Mary, I need a little more non-you right there." She moved back immediately and gave me my space. Matt grinned at the phrasing. I also wanted water but had not recovered enough motor skills to handle the glass, so I asked for my plastic bottle of water instead. From time to time when I raised it to my lips a body jolt would upset my aim and nearly dowse me.

I realized that as I was emerging from the general effects of the psilocybin I was also losing any chance for altered perceptions, much less the Beatific Vision. It did not seem likely I would reach any level of peace, and all I would be able to claim was that I had survived. I said that what I endured had been so severe that I would willingly sacrifice the opportunity to meet the Divine just to be back in ordinary reality. Matt told me this response was common among the program's volunteers and throughout all the literature on such experiences. It was a consolation to know not only that others felt the same way about escaping a bad situation but that they had not all reached transcendence either. Even having had a couple of surgeries, I couldn't remember undergoing anything so drastic in my life.

I told Matt, "This kind of a reaction has to be a self-defense method for the mushrooms that screams, 'Leave me alone and don't eat me!' " That struck me as a significant insight, but Matt said that one theory proposed that this hallucinogenic property might provide a natural protection from grazing animals.

It was then that I told Mary and Matt what I'd encountered after I returned from the depths. Except for the sense of the cobweb areas at the beginning, the passing notice of "the geometrics," the visit to my cells, and the vague appearance of light toward the end of the journey, nothing at all occurred that could be considered a hallucination. There had been no visions, no colors, and no changes in physical appearance when the eye mask was removed.

During this time Mary and Matt attempted to reintroduce the music quietly in the background, twice, but turned it off again when I asked. I still couldn't even bear to look at the room. I tried a few times but the sensations of sight were just too much to process. I was content to keep talking about anything and everything, like chores on my list, anecdotes, and my plans to rearrange the bookshelves in my living room. I sipped the water and kept shaking.

The spasms gradually eased into a rocking motion, and I found myself swaying forward and back or side to side. The movement was comforting in its way, and seemed to help dissipate the energy still pulsing through me. This kept on for what seemed like a couple of hours.

I remembered scenes of mentally disturbed people rocking their own bodies in their private worlds, and I felt a strong identity with them. A deep compassion arose toward persons in dire physical pain and anguish, particularly for those who would never recover from their condition as I hoped to improve from mine. It occurred to me even at the time that this empathy might be an enhanced reaction, but there was no way to distinguish how much of it was "original me" and how much could be attributed to the psilocybin. Nor did it seem to matter; the effect was the same.

My nose started to run, though I had no signs of a cold. I was guessing this was another method the body could use to purge the foreign substance. Mary brought me tissues when I asked, but I couldn't look around to find the box. I would just say, "Tissues!" and they would be put into my hands. "That's the way to live," I said, "State what you want to have, reach out your hand, and it appears."

After a little longer, I was able to open my eyes for increasing intervals. I asked what time it was — almost 3:00 p.m., they said. I had missed lunch and breaks while I was thoroughly occupied on other planes, in no condition to deal with anything else.

Mary offered me some grapes to help "bring me around," which was just the right incentive to make me reach for them. I was still rocking and sniffling, but definitely on the way back to the world I had left. About 4:00 p.m. I could finally put on my contact lenses and stand up again. When I was able to get to the bathroom, the ghastly image in the mirror showed I had aged ten years.

Mary and Matt welcomed me back to this world with a stack of questionnaires at the desk in the session room. It took some concentration to focus on them, both visually and mentally, but it was a good exercise. I recognized many of the same questions as in my original application; now perhaps different answers would be appropriate. However I still could not claim that I'd had an experience where I felt at one with the universe or had visions of saints or prophets, or had been uplifted in any way.

On the final question about what dose I thought I had received, I guessed medium high instead of high just in case I was mistaken to think it couldn't have been worse. After completing the questionnaires, I went back to sit on the couch, which looked normal and harmless after Matt and Mary had removed the sheets and replaced the cushions.

I was surprised when Dr. Griffiths came in again. I did not know that he had been receiving reports on my condition and that he always visited with the volunteer at the end of a session. Despite all the preparation and a strong dose of psilocybin, I had not reached a mystical state for their records or my own satisfaction, as such a high percentage of volunteers in the first study had reported. I didn't think he'd have any interest in my embarrassing performance, and was afraid he was going to scold me for bluffing that I knew anything about spirituality.

Dr. Griffiths quietly folded himself into a nearby chair. He took my hand, looked at me kindly and intently, and asked how the session had been for me. I did not understand why he appeared concerned at all, and I tried to keep my response brief because I was sure he was just putting in an appearance and wanted to be on his way. I told him I'd had "a rough ride," and was still having those lower-body tremors. I had seen no visions and met and conquered no demons.

When he asked about reactions of fear, I said no, meaning that I was not confronted by any of the psychological terrors I had been warned about. But I was clear that this had been far more harrowing than I could have imagined. I would rather spend three lifetimes sitting on a mountaintop trying to commune with the Divine than face another experience like that, I said. I had been through hell and had nothing to show for it.

I was sure Dr. Griffiths could see I was feeling shaken and inadequate, a disappointment to myself as well as to the States of Consciousness project, but he treated me like a dear friend he was glad to see again. I was pleased but confused by his solicitousness.

I had been worried that we were keeping Alida waiting. She was to have returned about 5:00 p.m. to pick me up, and now it was almost 6:00. When she was escorted up to the room she regaled Mary and Matt and Dr. Griffiths with the story of finding her way down to Baltimore's Inner Harbor and enjoying an afternoon in the shops.

After a short visit, the staff advised her that I might need some support that evening, and that there could be lingering effects from the psilocybin. They presented me with the red rose from the day's session and wished me well. When Mary walked me and Alida downstairs to the front door, she gave me her business card with her cell phone number written on the back and invited me to call her at any time if I needed. I would see them all again the next afternoon for the follow-up meeting.

It was a relief to be outdoors again and feel the fresh air on my face. I was still a little disoriented but knew I was going to return to normal life, and was delighted to be on solid ground — I would never again take it for granted. I felt like Ebenezer Scrooge discovering he was safely back in his room in time for Christmas Day.

We left the campus at twilight, stopping at a restaurant about half an hour later. Except for the grapes, I had not eaten since 7:00 a.m. I finished my salad, but found I could barely nibble at the large meal I had optimistically ordered, so I asked for a take-out box. Alida watched me clumsily scoop up a spoonful of dinner and plop it into the container, then she grabbed it all away from me good-naturedly and said, "Let me take care of that!" She scraped the food into the box in one definitive motion. I realized I still was not capable of even such a simple action, which both amused and dismayed me.

I did tell Alida that I had determined before I was even able to get up from the white couch that I had just finished my only psilocybin session with the Johns Hopkins program. I could not risk going through another such experience and would have to drop out of the study. They probably wouldn't miss me anyway after that debacle. I would be polite and go back for my meeting the next day, but there'd be no need to make any further trips to Baltimore.

God Gave Me a Stone

When the day was finally over and I was ready for bed in Alida's guest room about 10:00 p.m., I was afraid the session's physical sensations were going to come rushing back when I recreated the conditions of reclining in darkness. But it had to be done sooner or later, so I turned off the light and sank back on the pillow. It wasn't long before the spasms returned to trouble me, reminding that the psilocybin still could be working its way through my system. Two hours went by before the tremors subsided and I was able to fall asleep. I awoke again about 4:00 a.m., felt the jerks and shudders, and stayed awake for two more hours.

Lying there in the dark, I tried to review the whole experience. Certainly it had not been what I expected. They wanted hallucinogen-naïve, they *got* hallucinogen-naïve! It seemed I had failed the research team by not reaching a mystical state, and failed myself on the same count, plus causing a great deal of distress to my body. Yes, I had concerns when I agreed to explore that world, but I also had hope and trust. Now I felt I had wasted those people's time and resources and brought back not a single spiritual revelation. Obviously I couldn't transcend my way out of a paper bag.

But more important, I had hoped this would help me to approach the Divine Presence, to reach a level where further insights might be revealed to me, and it seemed I had been coldly denied. I found myself asking, "Dear God, I came to You so sincerely, with the purest intentions, and I cannot understand why I would be greeted this way. I traveled through hostile realms and beat upon your door in desperation, and You did not answer. How could that be? What did I do wrong? Show me where I failed and help me do better."

I remembered that, commending God's beneficence, Jesus had said, "What father when asked for bread by his son would give him a stone?" [6] I did not know why this had been my lot, but I had little perspective on the matter. Finding no answer, in time I fell asleep again, and was thankful not to have bad dreams or flashbacks.

I awoke about 8:00 the next morning with a mild headache. Alida and her husband were leaving the house for the day, and I needed to keep on schedule too. It was a fresh, bright morning, the very kind of weather I had wished for when I was emerging from the altered state, and I was outside in conventional reality (oh, blessed conventional reality!) to enjoy it. After breakfast at a fast-food restaurant, I sat in the back seat of my car with a clipboard and began to write up an account of the session to present to the staff at our afternoon meeting. From there I made the two-hour drive directly up to Baltimore.

CHAPTER 4

A Hesitant Return

At my appointment that afternoon, Mary and Matt greeted me with hugs and brought me into the interior room with the white couch, a room I would have been happy never to see again in my life. I knew I would be there only about an hour, and thought I could tolerate the confinement and unpleasant associations for such a short time. In an attempt at humor, I told them, "That was not the kind of experience I was hoping for. I want my money back." Matt laughed because I hadn't paid them a nickel. He joked, "We should give you *double* your money back!"

I read my handwritten report aloud at Mary and Matt's request. Despite the staff's cautions, I admitted, I had seriously underestimated the hallucinogen's power. My deepest regret was feeling that I had done a cruel injustice to my body. I am careful to get good nutrition, take vitamins, and have medical checkups, and then I bring on all this physical upset with psilocybin. Rather than fear, I added, the session had been characterized by a pervading feeling of helplessness.

However, Mary and Matt said it seemed as if the whole experience was fearful to me. They thought I may have had so much trouble because I'd struggled against impressions I perceived as threatening; if I had embraced them without resistance, the day may well have gone differently. As I saw it, my reaction was simply a primal instinct for survival, hard-wired into every organism. Maybe it *was* fear, but not the kind I expected. After their comments I lapsed into tears and began rocking back and forth. Neither of them seemed able to reassure me. When Mary asked how I felt, I could only answer, "Fragile."

I had been aware that psilocybin could cause some very unpleasant reactions, I told them, but did not remember being warned about any effects like those involuntary jolts. Mary acknowledged that some of the volunteers did have such tremors, and said that the staff would make a point of advising more clearly about the possibility. Well, no matter, I replied. Even if I had known about them, I would have swallowed the capsule anyway. There is no substitute for satisfying one's curiosity, and I really, really wanted that chance for transcendence. The previous day's events did not for a moment challenge my belief in a loving God or that someone can have a magnificent experience with entheogens.

Feeling fear while I was sinking into darkness and having spasms may not have been the highest response, but it seemed merely defensive, not wrong in the sense of intending harm. And if I did nothing wrong, why did I face such a battering? I would have thought the universe was more benign, and that whatever I encountered with psilocybin would be so plain as to make any interpretation unnecessary. (Eventually it occurred to me that my response may have been caused more by a physical reaction than a moral failing, though I still wondered about the possible relationship between them.)

I told Matt and Mary that I felt quite content to continue the path I was already on, feeling it was an appropriate one for me, and that I was willing to abandon any more bright ideas about taking a shortcut to enlightenment. I realized that I could not handle myself nearly so well in an altered reality as I would have thought, and was chastened to think I have a great deal of development ahead.

It was my understanding, I explained, that we all eventually have to go beyond our sense of self, our personality and ego identity, but I had expected to be attracted and welcomed into something better when that time came, not beaten up and left by the side of the road, as I felt in the psilocybin session. I said I wished I could have brought back more from my journey, though I knew I would contribute to their statistics one way or another, and "nothing is ever lost" nor in vain.

Matt and Mary were sympathetic and accommodating, despite all my protests and regrets. They gave me every consideration, and seemed genuinely grateful that I had volunteered to take the hallucinogen.

Another Interpretation

After my hour's meeting with them, Mary walked me down the hall to the office of Dr. Griffiths, who had already read my report from the session. When he greeted me, he took my hand in both of his, which seemed a very gracious gesture, and asked how I felt. I spoke up immediately about the unexpected spasms that had worried me during the session and recurred afterward. I also told him I was embarrassed to find myself rocking back and forth at the end of the session. "That's what crazy people do," I said, still too distraught to bother searching for some more subtle or politically correct phrase.

"Here in the West, when we see someone in such a state we usually medicate the person," Dr. Griffiths explained. "But in other cultures they might say, 'He's in an altered state,' and just respect the condition and monitor him." That sounded reasonable to me.

With tears welling up in my eyes, I described my sense of isolation during the night when I thought God had "given me a stone." This may have sounded like the depths of self-pity, yet it was all I could manage at the moment.

But Dr. Griffiths was not so quick to interpret this as a divine rejection. He quoted again the phrase from the Tibetan Book of the Dead: "Remember who you are, child of noble birth." It brought to mind one of my favorite passages from Bartholomew ("You are Light. You come from Light ... You have never been anything else..."),[7] and it was phrased so elegantly. Not only were these beautiful concepts, but they truly did sound correct.

I told Dr. Griffiths I remembered he had specifically warned that I might think I'd been given a higher dose than I was able to handle. I confessed that I had emerged feeling inadequate and self-critical, and that I was a disappointment to the research program, despite all the admonitions about any need to apologize. Also I was frank with my complaints that the music was imposing, though I didn't want to say too much about that and risk getting Matt and Mary in trouble for a breach of protocol when they turned it off. Besides, I knew I wasn't going to have to go through it again, a decision which I was not ready to share with Dr. Griffiths just then.

But when I reported I'd had no fear during the experience, he disagreed. "Yes, you did. You were in fear for 'my body, my precious body,' " demonstrating by clasping his arms across each other. He said that some psychological models would suggest that because of my concern for my physical safety I had not maintained an objective balance, which had kept me from rising above the immediate conditions. This might be regarded as a trick the ego used to resist being dissolved.

In my delicate emotional state, I was crushed to hear Dr. Griffiths offer this apparent criticism when I simply wanted comfort. There was no doubt I had miscalculated my abilities and what might happen if I did not abandon the ego, a concept I associated more with psychology than spirituality. Until just before the session, the staff had not mentioned ego in this context. I had no tutoring in how to identify it, why it might be a distraction, or how it could sabotage the experience. Nor was I convinced a person could set aside the ego without being in his right mind — it would be an accomplishment even then. But I could appreciate that by Dr. Griffiths' definitions I had indeed failed.

However, in our conversation he offered another possible interpretation. "Do you know what kundalini is?"

"Yes," I said. "The Hindu tradition describes it as the energy flow through two channels that wind upward around the spine, through the chakras, and it's represented as two snakes curving around the pole on the medical caduceus."

He nodded. Some observers might consider my involuntary movements to be evidence of a "kundalini awakening," he told me, a phrase he invited me to look up on the Internet. In Eastern settings, he went on, if someone felt a twitch or a jolt of energy when meditating, his companions would be a little curious or envious and ask, "How did you get that?" It would be considered a mark of advancement. This intrigued me.

I told Dr. Griffiths that so much I'd learned at Johns

Hopkins had shown me I needed to inquire more closely into Eastern philosophies. I also wanted to associate more with people I could talk with about general spiritual matters. He again recommended I explore the practice of meditation. He added that it would be interesting to see how I would react to a low dose of psilocybin (which implied even he thought I'd had a higher dose), and that he was sure I would "unpack" some further reflections as time went on. I was impressed not only with the breadth of his knowledge but his generosity in considering me capable of a kundalini awakening. He was beginning to seem much kinder and wiser than the chilly scientist I had first perceived.

After the meetings, I drove home congratulating myself on my decision not to remain in the program, but I was still reluctant to inform the staff, whom I liked well and who had invested so much in my preparation.

That evening I picked up one of my books by Bartholomew and suddenly remembered that Bart had referred to twitches in the nervous system. I found the passage with ease, and I saw a strong correlation when I reread a section I had highlighted years before:

> The doorways are in you, and you open them by choosing to. At present you have no idea of what is available to help you. You are not on this journey by yourself. If you think you are, I would give you a simple challenge — every day *give permission* to the energies that surround you to enter into your physical body, to transmute your old beliefs into new aware-ness, and to take the physical cells themselves and make them more radiant. Never in my experience have I found any human consciousness that reaches

and asks, on a continuing basis, to not be answered...

The gift those high frequency powers can give you is their intuitive knowledge of how much your physical body can stand. Too much voltage in your body at one time will burn out your circuits. It is not your diet that gets in the way, it is your belief systems that get in the way. You have accumulated an amazing amount of blockage, crystallization, and static through your belief systems, so when the energy starts moving into you, sometimes it feels painful. Sometimes you start to shake or twitch, or feel pain in different parts of your body. When you plug those higher frequencies in, you run right up against the old blockages of accumulated belief structures that act as a grid through which it is difficult for this energy to keep moving. So when you ask to be taught by these energies, they respond to you as you are ready to receive them, and you begin to make changes quietly, peacefully, and steadily.[8]

Not only did this seem to describe my unexpected assault, but it had been such an inspirational passage for me that I had routinely incorporated into my daily prayer an invitation for the higher energies to enter me physically. I was shocked to realize I had gotten my wish. Perhaps I should have specified, "Please come to me gradually, not like a herd of elephants when I'm vulnerable from a hallucinogen." If I had been more receptive and sought conscious attunement, the energies may have manifested more gently and slowly. But Bartholomew also points out that such expansion is easiest when we feel safe and relaxed, not exactly my situation during the psilocybin session.

"I Did It for You"

When I settled into my own bed that night, the abdominal spasms and leg movements awakened me about 1:00 a.m. Could the psilocybin still be affecting me a day and a half later, or was this something else entirely? I was able to return to sleep soundly, but the next morning when I awoke, the jolts were back, vivid reminders of the experience.

After breakfast, sitting at the table in my bathrobe, I found myself on the brink of tears, rocking back and forth, not at all ready to turn my attention to practical matters. My original appraisal of the risks had not included any information about the prolonged shaking, so I felt I had unintentionally put myself in harm's way.

I idly said a conscious "thank you" to the body for undergoing the session two days earlier. I was surprised to get a strong physical reaction with a wave of emotion that set me crying again. A few minutes later I recognized this as a distinct message that could be translated into words. The body had responded lovingly, "I did it for you. This is my gift to you." I do not usually get messages this way, but it was delivered with a convincing intensity.

Mary phoned later that morning out of personal concern. I was so grateful to hear her voice that I sat and sobbed. She tried to reassure me, and said that the psilocybin would have passed out of my system by then, which left no explanation for my tenuous emotional and physical condition. I spent the rest of the day in quiet recovery, getting myself back together.

That night I was awakened again by the spasms and seemed to feel a mild return of an altered state. The following day I wanted nothing more than to be quiet and contemplate. Sometimes I still found myself rocking and crying. But I needed to go out to get a few things, so I tried to remember how one interacted with store clerks and how to make casual conversation. I was relieved to get home again afterward.

There were more tremors as I fell asleep that evening, during the night, and again the next morning, and I began to wonder if I'd incurred some actual nerve damage. As I lay there waking up slowly, I tried to assess them objectively. Though worrisome and abnormal, the shudders didn't hurt. They had been occurring in my abdomen and legs only. I was thrilled to think this might be evidence of kundalini energy, but also disappointed that only the lower areas were affected. Maybe my base chakras were so blocked that no upward progression was possible.

A little analysis showed that the jolts had consistently originated from a single point since their onset. It felt as if someone were yanking a string attached to one particular place in my abdomen, setting off contractions that involved my legs only as a follow-through. It was always the same spot, in the back toward the spine, no farther up than my second chakra. Then I suddenly remembered. "Wait a minute! There *is* one special area there that has its own name, a word that starts with H." I jumped out of bed and began to pull books off my shelf until I found the illustration. The spasms were emanating from my *hara*.

I read that the *hara*, a Japanese term, is a center of power in the lower belly, containing a more defined area called the *tan tien* (or *dantien*). It is said to be the one note that holds the physical body in manifestation, and a harmonic of the sound made by the molten core of the earth. This level of the subtle body corresponds to our intentionality.[9] Perhaps the psilocybin activated my *hara* like an initiation, I thought, or the center provided an essential link to keep me grounded. Maybe it was just a screaming complaint from my nervous system. In any case, I was glad to have the reference.

As the week went on, I felt a strong need to be alone and assimilate the experience, and was thankful I didn't have to leave the house or talk with anyone. I admired volunteers with jobs and families who could manage their obligations, when I found it difficult to go out and take care of errands even three days later.

A few close friends who knew about my participation in the program asked about the psilocybin session. "How was it? What happened?" I told them they could duplicate the sensation very easily. Drink a bottle of rum, a bottle of vodka, and a bottle of tequila. Get into a barrel and have someone nail down the lid and throw you over Niagara Falls. The descent should last three or four hours, then they should let you churn around at the bottom of the falls for a few more hours before they fish you out. Except for the recovery, that's pretty much it. I felt that no threat, no reward, no desire to help science or please those lovely people could make me voluntarily take another dose.

I rebuked myself for having confidently elbowed my way into the States of Consciousness project and then demonstrated that I was a total novice. Just because I had an interest in theological subjects didn't mean I had any facility in them. I couldn't distinguish my deeper identity, the "I Am" observer, from the personality, so there wasn't much hope of learning to set aside the ego on short notice. Without that ability or a better understanding of the operating rules of alternate realities, it seemed reckless to take the risk of another such confrontation, or something even worse. Mary had said, "It's different every time," which confirmed that the experience would be unpredictable.

I did genuinely like the staff and, naturally, all the attention. I loved associating with academic professionals who could speak with familiarity on spiritual matters. Mary was warm and supportive, Matt had a wide knowledge of drugs and their effects, and I looked forward to my talks with Dr. Griffiths, who always offered something relevant to consider. Mary and Matt referred to him simply as "Roland," but no one, including he himself, was inviting me to be so casual. At the very least, his crisply ironed shirts and coordinated ties justified the more formal address.

As I slowly returned to my regular functions, I drew up a list of conditions under which I would consider taking a second dose of psilocybin, though I did not think it was likely that the researchers would agree to my terms (or negotiate with terrorists): (1) I must be guaranteed the dose would be low; (2) There must be either no music or music chosen by me; (3) The session would not be held in that interior room; and (4) If I were to take another dose, it couldn't be soon. I needed time to process the experience and prepare better.

"I'm Supposed to Be Here"

Another visit with the staff was scheduled nine days after the session. This time I happily accepted their offer to meet in a different room, a small, plain office with a couch and a window. Since I had "unpacked" so many further reflections, I asked if I could bring a more detailed written report.

I suspected that Mary and Matt could sense my reluctance to proceed. Other volunteers may have had similar challenges,

I thought. Those in the first study had received a single dose of psilocybin. However, in the second study a dozen ahead of me had multiple doses, and perhaps some of them had felt overwhelmed too. So I flatly asked, "What's your dropout rate?" When Mary told me no one had chosen to leave, I wondered how I had been accepted along with so many brave and capable people.

Mary and Matt gave me every consideration in making my own decision. I would have felt more encouraged to continue if they'd said they saw some potential in me or described again my efforts to qualify or if they'd painted a glowing picture of the mystical state I might reach, but they did not offer any comment or opinion.

I inquired about having the session somewhere else, but that wasn't practical because the cameras and the sound equipment were installed in the interior room. I was hoping there might be some way to negotiate about the music soundtrack, but the oblique questions and answers about this with Matt and Mary showed that the program administrators controlled this decision. Their trump card was always "protocol." All the volunteers had to undergo the same conditions in order for the results of the research to be statistically useful.

By this time I was beginning to recover physically from the effects of the session. The spasms still occurred under certain conditions but were no longer a source of fear. I told Mary that even if Dr. Griffiths had not made the correlation with the movement of kundalini energy, I would probably have come to regard them as harmless. They seemed less worrisome if I thought of them as *surges* of energy, I said, not a neurological problem. I was reestablishing my emotional equilibrium, too, and was less likely to break down in tears.

Although changes in the routine seemed unlikely, I had to admit I still felt privileged to be a part of the study. The staff had been sympathetic and patient, and I knew that this was a once-in-a-lifetime opportunity. My course of action became clear. I told Mary and Matt that I would remain in the program. I just plain wanted to know about other realms and the nature of God, and if this amazing substance, this point of access from the natural world, could reveal anything to me then I would try it again. I realized I had learned valuable lessons from the first session, miserable as it was, and a great deal from my association with the staff at Johns Hopkins.

"I'm supposed to be here," I told them. My intuition said as much. There was an element of surrender on my part, but also satisfaction in recognizing that the decision was the right one. Mary quietly took my hand and said, "Yes, I know you're supposed to be here, too. We honor your choice."

However, I did ask for one modification. The next session was scheduled in less than three weeks, and I didn't feel ready to face it. Could we delay it for a month? Mary and Matt agreed to the postponement, and I was grateful. Everything else would remain the same.

When I met with Dr. Griffiths that day, I brought a cartoon I had drawn of him on the phone saying, "Hello, pharmacy? We've got another one of those cocky volunteers down here. Send over a high dose … heh-heh-heh." I wasn't sure how he'd regard that, but he seemed amused and reminded me that because the study was double-blind, he himself had no information on what dosage the volunteer received.

About ten days after that, I had another routine appointment with Matt and Mary, who suggested we again hold our meeting in the room with the window. As we talked about my reactions, I said that I'd felt so helpless during the psilocybin session partly because I couldn't see anything in the altered state. The darkness corresponded to the insecurity and defensiveness we feel in our everyday world when we can't maneuver in confidence or know what may be lying in wait for us. I had expected at least to see lights and colors to verify that I was responding normally to the hallucinogen. I was honestly surprised when Matt replied that many people don't experience any visual effects during the activity of psilocybin.

Back in Mary's office after the meeting, I balanced a clipboard on my lap and set to work filling out the stack of questionnaires required three weeks after every psilocybin session. Mary had told me in advance to allow about two hours for the task.

I had answered many of the same questionnaires, if not all, during my application and immediately after my psilocybin session. This time I scribbled down the names of the sets on a scrap of paper for my journals: Persisting Effects; Feelings, past week; Death Transcendence Scale; FACIT (V.4); FMS; LOT-R; M Scale: Form A; Measure of Actualization of Potential; The PANAS-X; Quality of Life Inventory; Spiritual Transcendence Scale; Satisfaction with Life Scale; and the grand finale, clicking off the answers to 241 questions while sitting at Mary's computer. By my count, the total for the day came to 700.

Answers to most of these were either yes/no or a choice from five gradations. One of the more elaborate questionnaires offered the oddly worded choices: Extremely true / Quite a bit true / Moderately true / A little bit true / Cannot decide / A little bit not true / Moderately not true / Quite a bit not true / Extremely not true. Sometimes a positive question was followed by one with similar negative wording, or even a double negative, so I had to think twice about whether my answers should swing to the other end of the scale. I was asked again whether I'd lost all sense of time and space, or felt one with God. Did I feel love for my fellow man, or fear, depression, aggression? But my responses had not changed much since I'd completed the previous batch.

For many of these I wished there were some provision for me to specify whether I was proud of my answer ("I enjoy philosophical discussions") or whether I was acknowledging it with apologies ("I am not always a cheerful person"). Others seemed far too complex to be answered by circling a number. When I'd face one like, "After death, much of myself lives on through my children," I would complain to Mary, "No fair! These are essay questions!"

As I finished various sections, Mary would look them over to make sure they were complete. When she noticed I had qualified my answers to two successive questions, she asked me to explain the distinctions and made notations in the margin. I thought this was being a little too literal, but I respected their careful review.

I was glad I had brought a bottle of orange juice to this 10:00 appointment because by the time I was ready to meet with Dr. Griffiths it was after 2:00. When he came to Mary's office to talk with me, she gave him this paperwork and pointed out the two answers where I had been less than decisive. He took a moment to check over those discrepancies with me. I wanted to let him know it was not that important to me, really; I simply could have changed my answers to fit their model. But instead I made a mental note that they *did* notice and it would be easier just to do things their way.

I told Dr. Griffiths I was still having some of those occasional muscle spasms, but now they occurred only when I was in repose — either falling asleep or waking, reflecting, or sitting in meditation. I described a recent occasion when I had arrived home one night, enjoying a symphony on the car radio. When I stopped in my driveway, I sat there in the dark to listen to the rest of the piece. As soon as I relaxed into it, the surges began. They ceased when I diverted my attention from the music to the physical sensation, but the moment I focused on the music again, they returned. I said I had come to think of the surges as indicators that I was changing levels of consciousness. I expected them to fade completely as the energies stabilized over time, and in fact, I added, I would kind of miss them.

Dr. Griffiths seemed to approve when I told him I was trying to establish a personal practice of meditation, persisting through many lapses of attention. He advised that sometimes even an experienced meditator can be so distracted and unable to control thought during meditation that to sit there at all serves as a testament of sincerity. I always appreciated his comments and knew there was much I could learn from him, but his schedule allowed me only 15 minutes.

As Mary walked me downstairs and out into the mild afternoon, we chatted as friends. I learned that she had a Masters in Social Work, had been a school counselor, and was volunteering with a hospice organization. Mary said she had joined the staff of the States of Consciousness Research Project at the suggestion of Dr. Richards, an acquaintance from her meditation group. I was glad to find out a little about her background to help balance our relationship.

Whenever I was talking with the staff, I made it a point to

note any subjects or books they cited so I could share the same references. One of these was the movie *Fierce Grace*, which I rented and watched too. It featured some historic black-and-white footage from the life of Richard Alpert before he became known as Ram Dass. The film also showed Timothy Leary expounding on his theories, and some modern-day interviews with Huston Smith. This gave me valuable information on the drug culture of the 1960s. I was in college then, but almost oblivious to that movement. Decades would pass before I, too, would be swallowing a capsule. It was fascinating to see images of these famous men on film and to think that I was continuing in their footsteps, though their version of hallucinogen research had little in common with the methods used at Johns Hopkins.

Giving Brahms His Due

At the end of October Mary and Matt arranged a special meeting to help desensitize me to the music that had upset me so much in the first session. They also wanted to acclimatize me more to that interior session room that I found stuffy and claustrophobic.

I had been preparing for this visit with some meditations to relax and work with whatever was presented. Mary explained that they could not eliminate or substitute the music, so I was sure I would meet tough resistance if I tried to evade it again.

I stepped into the session room bravely that day, trying not to reveal my concerns. During the talk that began our meeting, I said that when some previous intestinal difficulties had returned recently, I had doubted my physician's guess that I might have diverticulitis. Instead I found a salon for several professional colonic cleansings, which made a significant improvement. I expected the treatment to also help me better assimilate the psilocybin at the next session.

Matt had brought a photocopied page from a scientific study, a chart showing various psychoactive substances rated for both toxicity and dependence.[10] He wanted to assure me that psilocybin was physically one of the safest and had the lowest potential for addiction.

After a half-hour of conversation, it was time to lie down on the white couch and confront the forceful music that I had been dreading. I proposed a deal: if Mary and Matt would let me forego the headphones and just listen to the music from the speakers across the room, I would let them roll out the most ponderous, heavy-duty pieces in their arsenal. We could even start right in the middle and skip all the pleasantries. However, that's what they had planned to do anyway. I listened to the speakers at first, then when they asked that I put on the headphones, I complied quietly.

Late morning is when the activity of psilocybin reaches its peak, so the music is timed to get progressively more "strongly structured" (as Dr. Richards later described it) up to that point. I hadn't heard anything further because I'd begged for the music to be turned off, but Matt and Mary told me the programming became much more gentle after that. Since there seemed to be no way out of this rehearsal, and the music was going be directed right into my headphones, I had no alternative. I knew I could feel stressed even without hallucinogens; the music would suffice very well.

Mary and Matt queued up the track that had scared me out of my wits in the psilocybin session. They identified it as the opening of Brahms' Symphony No. 1, which was not familiar to me before the research project. Heavy drumbeats advanced like enemy footsteps, threatening me with painful and grisly annihilation. I couldn't remember ever hearing anything more driving, menacing, and viscerally brutal. Every nerve was on edge.

I tried to observe the music impartially as a sequence of harmless sounds. The opening bars with the drumbeat were the most fearful, then the tone evened out a bit. By the time the pounding came up again it was not so insistent, and would fade away. I had survived, at least for the moment.

One other selection from the early hours of the soundtrack was particularly troublesome, a choral work about fifteen minutes long, and I had to listen to the entire piece again there in the meeting. But I needed to confront this issue seriously or I couldn't hope to deal with the music while the hallucinogen was active.

I looked at the title Mary showed me later and neither of us could guess at its translation. It was Brahms again, *Denn alles Fleisch* from his German *Requiem*. The recording had great subtlety and balance on the part of the orchestra and chorus, but I remembered its foreboding only too well from the first session. I could picture Charon poling me across the Styx, or a torchlit medieval procession.

I asked Mary and Matt, "What do you think Dr. Richards had in mind? Why would he pick that instead of something lyrical and lofty? Maybe a little Mozart would lift the spirits better than such frightening pieces."

They told me that Dr. Richards did not choose all of the program, it was a collaborative effort with others. The soundtrack had provided a standard background for each session in the first study with 36 volunteers, and now for this second study. Matt said that many of the early hallucinogen experiments had incorporated music as part of their process. He theorized that the authors of this research program may have been using music to mirror an individual's personal struggle, the build-up and resolution of tensions that can precede a transcendental state.

I knew that even if I were able to meet the music with more confidence it could be draining. However, I did have the advantage of rehearsing it a couple of times, including the first psilocybin session itself, so I knew it wouldn't get any more extreme than that. I still had my doubts about the adversity theory, and maintained that one could go straight to heaven without a detour through hell.

I remembered that when the changes in consciousness had begun they were so swift and powerful that I had to hurry to get into position with the headphones and eye mask before I was lost in the maelstrom. So I told Mary and Matt that for the next session I would like to lie down immediately after taking the capsule, to just be quiet and have time to collect and center myself before the effects began.

Mary hesitated and said, "Well, I don't know. That isn't part of the protocol, and we'd have to ask Roland if we could make that adjustment. We always have the person sit for a while and talk or look at a book because it's going to be at least twenty minutes before the psilocybin becomes active." I could see that if such a small variation required approval, then dispensing with the music entirely would be impossible.

I described to Matt and Mary an exercise where I had tried to find advantages to having the session in the interior room. To counter my claustrophobia, I had imagined being escorted into a secure area and then on to an inner sanctum like the

Holy of Holies that few were allowed to enter, a place where I was so completely protected that I could abandon all fears. They thought that was a creative approach. What I didn't say was that I was still not convinced by it.

After our meeting, which had lasted almost two hours, I met with Dr. Griffiths, who glanced at his watch and said he had only about five minutes for me. We briefly discussed my reaction to the music and I told him I was doing my best to regard it with equanimity. That happened to be a word he liked, and he suggested I meet everything in life with that very equanimity.

He inquired whether I had located a meditation group, which I had not, but I mentioned that I found myself taking issue with some instructions in a book on meditation I was reading. He explained that the practice includes every possible variation in method. Some schools allow meditation in any position, including standing or lying down; others, he said, insist on only a "full lotus." He advised not getting too caught up in the techniques, but to consider the practice openly and humbly as a beginning student. Then he checked the time again and said a quick goodbye.

Last-Minute Cramming

On the way home, and for a few days afterward, I began to develop some reservations about the program. I had always admired these people and sought their approval, but now I found myself questioning whether their inflexible procedures were making the situation more difficult than necessary. The staff had repeatedly advised me to approach altered states without expectation, yet it seemed the music was designed to channel the volunteer into carefully scripted emotional responses. I wasn't so sure I couldn't have found a better route by myself. How might the experience be different if I took a natural hallucinogen with a shaman in the utter silence of a cold desert night?

If they'd change the music, not play the same program for every psilocybin session, I thought, then the person could have a more spontaneous experience without anticipating the next step. But then, that wouldn't be a strict protocol, would it. While I was grousing about the intractable arrangements, they were probably getting a little annoyed with me too. Their entire project was set up to provide data under carefully controlled conditions, and they couldn't afford to invalidate it with variances just because one of the volunteers was snivelling.

If nothing else, this meeting had made it blazingly clear that I would have to find some way to deal with the Brahms pieces before my next session in only two weeks. There was no room for negotiation. I ordered both the symphony and the *Requiem*, and bought some headphones, too. While waiting for the CDs to be delivered, I went to an online retail site and clicked to listen to the opening of the symphony, then tried to bravely withstand it. Only the first thirty seconds played out, but that was the worst, right there. I went through it over and over, amazed that it always seemed so terrifying when I knew exactly what to expect and had purposely chosen it.

The CDs arrived just a few days before the next session was scheduled. I practiced by lying on my sofa in the dark with the headphones. As soon as the music began, my fear returned with a fresh intensity. Even after listening to it a number of times, the memory of the original experience and echoes of the same physical reactions remained. How was it going to be with a hallucinogen warping my mind? This was like cramming for an exam. I wrote in my journals that I would never have guessed this five-session program would have been so complicated and demanding, and that I might not have applied if I had understood the details, particularly about the music. I did not hold out much hope for being able to dismiss my ego on cue, yet I realized I do it readily every night when I fall asleep. I knew if I could keep in mind Joel Goldsmith's declaration that "there is only one power," if I could survive the next round of psilocybin without being sidetracked again, I would be far better off for my participation.

It did bring a sense of accomplishment to recognize that I was extending beyond my previous limits. Although I was cautious and a little frightened, I was drawn onward out of curiosity and a desire to learn more. It wasn't so much a sense of service to mankind, because I didn't see how such a small sample of volunteers could demonstrate much of a pattern to the researchers. But that was their bailiwick, not mine.

My immediate goal was simply to survive the full music program during the next session, no matter what dosage I received. In an email to Mary about a week before the session I said that I was trying hard to prepare for it. With tongue in cheek I added I was not sure whether on such short notice I could complete my agenda of surrendering the ego and mastering illusion and fear, though I would report for duty in any case. Mary replied that my standards were so high that if I were in charge not a single volunteer would qualify for the study. I took her generally sunny response as an acknowledgement of my good intentions. I *was* trying to take full advantage of the opportunity. And the days were rapidly counting down to the next session.

CHAPTER 5

Dancing With the Light

On a Tuesday morning in mid-November my alarm went off at 4:30 a.m. and the excitement began again. This time I drove an hour to the home of my sister Lisa, and then it took us over two hours to reach the Bayview campus in Baltimore.

I arrived with fewer props this time, but not fewer fears. After signing in at the front desk and being escorted upstairs, I provided a urine sample for the drug check and waited in Mary's office while she was setting up the room. Dr. Griffiths spent some time with me offering assurances and reviewing the importance of not resisting the way the session would unfold. He even advised I would weather the psilocybin experience much better if I confidently invited it to "Give me your best shot!" But remembering my impaired reasoning the previous time, I told him I could not promise I would be successful.

After being escorted through the labyrinth of doors and hallways, and after the preliminary blood pressure check, I took my place in the center of the couch as the three staff members gathered around to offer me the brown goblet with a single, deceptively plain capsule at the bottom. This was a pivotal moment, but I had no doubts about my decision. I washed down the capsule with a drink of water, feeling both noble and foolhardy. "The whole glass of water," they instructed. "Finish the whole glass."

After Dr. Griffiths returned to his office, Mary and Matt sat beside me on the couch to look at an art book until the psilocybin took effect. In about fifteen or twenty minutes, when I was sure I had received an active dose, they helped me with the eye mask, the headphones, the blanket, and the blood pressure cuff, and I began to sink into another world.

The descent seemed even rougher than the previous time, a rattling, lurching, high-speed roller coaster ride straight downhill through tingling geometric symbols and tunnels of textured blackness. The music on the soundtrack exaggerated the eerie atmosphere and kept me wary. Once again the abdominal spasms started up as well. Chemicals washed over me in a series of waves, sending a spicy heat through my body and leaving a bad taste in my mouth. As soon as I regained my balance after one of these, another would begin to course through my system.

However, there were significant differences that tempered the experience. Most obviously, I had been through this before. Although I found the passage of entry unnerving, with its sensations of being overpowered, I recognized landmarks so there was a useful frame of reference. I remembered the feeling of falling and going through tunnels, I remembered the flashing shapes, and I remembered the music. Even the two Brahms pieces I'd worried about just flew by while I was occupied with the changes, and I didn't have time to be frightened by them. If anything, noticing that part of the soundtrack offered a bit of comfort — "Ah, yes, I know those bad boys!"

I had forgotten another impression from the first session,

emerging into "rooms" or public areas in the blackness. Some-times I seemed to be on the periphery of a large sphere, many stories tall, with a city-of-the-future feel to it, tiers of terraces around the edge and flying objects like space cars. For all I knew, this could have been a single atom — all proportion was lost. I described the scene to Mary and Matt so it wouldn't escape the records again.

Despite the strong effects of the psilocybin, I was able to keep in mind my intention to work with what was presented to me. Whenever my consciousness regrouped into my familiar identity, I mentally repeated, "Tell me where we are going. I am willing to follow where you lead." I was determined to remain as cooperative and nonjudgmental as possible, even though I was apprehensive.

Before the session had begun that morning, I had re-quested that Bartholomew, Joel Goldsmith, and the Archangel Michael help me through the experience. Now when I silently called on them to come and be with me, I detected a wry amusement as if they had been watching. "We are already here," they responded wordlessly. "It is *you* who are in *our* territory now." I told this to Mary and she too found it sur-prising. As I felt the truth of their message, it heartened me.

At last the descent ceased and I reached a point of stability, even though nothing in particular emerged as a next stage. Perhaps an hour or two had passed. Unlike my previous session with psilocybin, my mind was functioning clearly, and I had a mild feeling of suspense. I was deeply immersed in that reality, but mentally alert, when I told Mary I needed to go to the bathroom. I thought if I could just get that simple dis-traction out of the way, I could devote my full attention to the inner activities.

Glorious Light!

Mary obligingly took off my headphones and eye mask in preparation for getting me up from the couch. When I tried to rise to a sitting position, I found myself heavy and dizzy — my mind and emotions were steady, but the body was not as co-operative. The soft light of the room's lamps glared on my dilated pupils, so I chose to lie down again and cover my eyes until they adjusted.

After a few minutes, instead of getting accustomed to the level of light, it seemed that the light was becoming brighter and brighter and strangely *brighter*, until I came to realize that this light was not in the room, it was inside me. At that moment, it was as if all the cylinders in the lock somehow fell into alignment, the door swung open, and I found my awareness being flooded with brilliant Light. Without notice or fanfare I had arrived at a transcendental state and was awestruck at the discovery. I felt a joyous expansion as it opened fully to me, like entering a splendid palace, yet the feeling was completely natural and gentle.

With my eyes closed I was overwhelmed with glorious golden light suffused with color, prisms and rainbows everywhere like a shining hologram. The Light itself was alive, a radiant consciousness of ultimate intelligence, perfect integrity, singularity and purity. The Light composed everything. It pervaded everything. Its presence was benevolent, calm, and intense.

It was as if the Light were revealing to me the innermost workings of the universe. Without words, It informed me that It was the source of all physical manifestation and that each event and object had its purpose: "Everything is in My perfect keeping. With this as Cause, there can be no mistakes." I knew

It to be the substance of every particle in the microcosm and the overarching essence of the macrocosm. In that moment I intuitively understood how all things are being created continuously from Its emanation. Why, then, could we not see the Light permeating all of creation? How could the shining substance of all things be hidden? Later I recalled the classic explanation of the sages: the only possible answer is that our sense perceptions are an illusion.

Faced with the reality and the wonder of the Light, I could only gape with the greatest reverence. There are no questions in Its Presence, no desires, no resistance. I felt suspended in a serene and peaceful state, a weightless free-fall without time and space. Even my physical surges abated, as if their purpose had been accomplished. Occasionally I still felt a faint muscle spasm, like the echo of receding thunder.

As I was poised there, rapt and transparent, the Light spoke directly: "Is there anything you want?" The question to me was forthright, yet it seemed incongruous because my whole identity was already absorbed in that Light. To search for an answer, I had to make a deliberate effort to turn my attention to the world from which I'd come, a place now distant and irrelevant. With a moment's focus I remembered that life on earth required healing and guidance and abundance, and that I had many wishes there. But I felt so removed from that personality, and I didn't want to look away from the Light for even an instant. The question was addressed to the one who stood before it in this exceptional experience, and there could be only one response. I breathed the quietest possible, "No, there is nothing I want."

I didn't know what to do in the presence of this Light. It glowed peaceably, with no conditions. I was just basking in it and, again, trying to remain open to all possibilities. And yet, I could also observe It independently and report back to Mary and Matt. I wanted to shout, "It *is* true! It *does* exist!" Sometimes in a dream there is a sense that whatever you try to name or record will evaporate, but this experience in the Light remained steady as I tried to describe it, even though I was a little concerned that my sharing it might be sacrilegious and It would withdraw.

The power of the Light could have annihilated me in an instant, but It shone only as brightly as my consciousness could bear. The Divine seemed to lovingly limit Its manifestation to what my own self-imposed definitions could perceive. Like the story of the fisherman and the mermaid, there was an understanding that as long as I maintained a human identity we could not be joined in ultimate communion. The limitations were plainly mine, but the shared feelings of affection, yearning and respect remained. The unspoken promise was that one day I would return with sufficient mastery to lay down my illusions, and the separation would be resolved.

And so, with nothing else to be done, we danced. That is as good a description as any. The Light waxed and waned, perhaps mirroring the processes of the psilocybin. It would shine brightly, then recede, leaving me in repose, peaceful and floating. Again It would return more strongly. It caressed me, holding me in the palm of Its hand, so to speak, with exquisite tenderness and compassion. My eyes brimmed with tears of emotion as I was poised in this timeless state.

The Light spoke to me in the language of every human relationship — as if I were a child, a friend, and a lover. It told me It was pleased at my efforts to find It, and that It acknowledged my sincerity. At times the Light was playful, and we carried on nearly in giggles as if we had a secret. I teased Mary saying, "It's like I'm on a private phone conversation with It, and you can't hear!" The Light and I continued that give-and-take rhythm, like a graceful and spontaneous duet.

My body maintained its own perspective, rejoicing that for these moments I could perceive that which constantly creates and supports it. With the Light, I visited a basic, formative physical level, where I had observed the cells in my first psilocybin session, so the Light could refresh and invigorate those processes. I was not a participant in this activity, although I had to agree to it, because the Light and the cells shared a language which my conscious Self did not comprehend. Matt reminded me the next day that I said I had watched It tapping my cells like a wand on a pod, opening each of them to reveal the natural light inside and showing them how to heal themselves. The experience was so convincing that after the session I was disappointed to find my chronically poor eyesight was not improved.

In another scenario, I knew that an immense power might be released when two wings were spread over me. I was prepared for the impact and felt no fear, but the wings drew back without imparting any change. If they had not, I suspect all my physical circuitry would have been overloaded and some function may have been damaged.

There was one other notable and curious event. As this direct perception of the Light began to draw to a close, I felt as if a special charge of energy was being stored in my abdomen for strength I would need. Then it seemed a "program" was being implanted there, too, some additional ability or access that would be activated at an unspecified future time. I was not told its purpose, but I was assured that there was nothing I needed to do — all would be taken care of by its designers. My function is merely to be the host. I do not recall being asked for my consent, but when the Light wants Its way, there is nothing to say but yes. I hoped that when this happened, perhaps a matter of years, I would remember its origin.

And so the Light drifted away for longer and longer intervals, and told me It would miss me as we slowly parted. I tried to observe how It looked and felt so I could capture every detail of the vision. Even then I was wondering how difficult it would be to find It again at any time in my earthly life. But I told Matt and Mary tearfully, "I will always remember that it is *possible*."

Once you have seen this Light, a deep recognition verifies that it is as powerful and moving as all the accounts testify. Even though it cannot be documented or proven, it is a one-hundred-percent convincing experience that so indelibly imprints the psyche that you declare, "Previously I knew it only intellectually, but now I am certain it is real."

Mary and Matt let me loll on the couch without my eye mask for most of this time, and with the headphones removed I could even enjoy lying on my side while the ethereal music from the speakers helped keep me aloft. I was aware that this was the much-sought transcendental experience that psilocybin could occasion, and I was continually amazed that I could have a split-screen version of physical and mystical realities at the same time. I kept my eyes closed most of the time, but whenever I glanced at the room, I saw that Mary and Matt were occupied with reading and paperwork. They remained quiet, responding only when I spoke first.

When it was clear that the effects were diminishing, I finally did get up for that trip to the bathroom. I felt so groggy that I could hardly walk. Mary and Matt were right at my side to steady me and guide me to the door.

I learned that all these events had transpired in only three hours. I returned to the couch for several hours more with the headphones and the eye mask at the request of my guides. When I reclined again, the physical sensations of dizziness subsided and my interior world became the dominant reality once more. Although I was peaceful and still enjoyed the feeling of expansion, I did not see the Light again.

A Slow and Pleasant Return

My return to conventional waking consciousness seemed long and slow, but fairly pleasant, unlike the desperate spasms and rocking that characterized the first session. I would share an occasional comment with Mary and Matt, then just lie there, physically spent. Sometimes I was speaking so softly that Mary had to stay close to discern my words, then I could hear her whispering to Matt for his notes. I waved my hand around and said, "High dose, Mary! Put me down for the high dose today!" I said I hoped I *did* have flashbacks. I also blithely informed Matt that his Ph.D. would be of absolutely no use in that realm.

As my focus returned to the room, I again reached the transition point where I craved fresh air, cold water and outdoor spaces, but I could be more patient this time. After a little while I was ready to try to sit up and open my eyes, able to resume life as I had known it with greater ease than on the first occasion two months before.

Because I was so much more lucid during this session, I had an opportunity to pay close attention to the audio program that had been interrupted during my first disastrous day on the couch. The opening selections were lovely and charming, but as the psilocybin began to take effect, the well-timed musical cues evolved into a tone that was ominous, mysterious, rumbling. It evened out after another hour or so as the action of psilocybin reached its peak, and transposed into some of the most beautiful pieces in the western classical repertoire.

As the effects of the entheogen began to wane in the afternoon, the music changed to reflect the return to the everyday world. Toward the end of the session it became grounded again with earthy songs by John Lennon, Louis Armstrong, and a gospel choir, plus a selection or two of Indian sitar music similar to one from the morning. By the time I was ready for the questionnaires, the soundtrack ended with a soothing background of ocean waves.

Responding to those familiar written questions, at last I could provide some new answers. But I was still unable to say yes to whether I had ever perceived myself to be at one with all creation. I had read about the principle many times, but had not personally experienced it.

When Dr. Griffiths returned at the end of the day, he seemed pleased that the session had gone well. He held out the red rose in the vase and inquired earnestly about my perceptions of it. I misinterpreted his question and replied that I always appreciated the beauty of nature. What he was asking instead, I later realized, was how the rose appeared to my senses. But I had no altered visual perceptions during this or the previous psilocybin session, and I had no hallucinations.

My sister Lisa was brought up to join us, warmly welcomed and introduced around. It was not lost on me that when Mary said, "And this is Dr. Griffiths," he smiled, offered Lisa his hand, and softly corrected, "Roland." If he would invite this new acquaintance to use his first name, then perhaps he had given me the same privilege, and I had not remembered.

During the trip home, with a stop for dinner, Lisa was very sociable, talking about her day, when I would have preferred to be quiet or discuss my experience. But I would have the rest of my life to reflect on it, so I continued the discipline of dealing with whatever presented itself.

After saying goodnight to Lisa's family at her home, I sat at their computer to capture my recollections of the day's events. I knew that this might be the only occasion in my life when that dimension of light was open to me, and I wanted to preserve everything I could remember. I printed out the pages to take to the staff for my report the next day.

When I finally went to bed, I was hoping to drift again into an altered state, but fell right asleep after having been up almost 20 hours. I awakened a few times during the night with a headache and a touch of nausea, but neither was strong enough to require even an over-the-counter remedy.

"I Am Amazing"

The next day I made the trek back to Baltimore from Lisa's, even farther than the drive from my home, for my scheduled afternoon meeting with the staff. Instead of the personal concerns I often heaped on Matt and Mary, this time I walked in with a smile and said, "I was so looking forward to coming here today to bring you my joy!" Mary replied, "But Maria, you always bring us your joy."

We held our meeting in the inner room with the white couch; obviously there were no further unhappy associations. I told Matt and Mary I believed that I was able to physically

access a transcendental state more easily because I had endured
the first dose of psilocybin. Since I had a better idea of what to
expect, I could concentrate instead on Dr. Griffiths' coaching
to let go and be carried wherever the experience took me. I had
resolved to remember my instructions, and willingly went
where I was led.

And then the Light had dawned unexpectedly. It seemed
more than just "light," I said. It was a consciousness with power
and presence and intensity. Like a laser, it was a coherent light,
I told Matt, which I thought was the scientific term for wave
alignment. It wasn't just shining light. It was concentrated,
purposeful, *intelligent* light.

Matt checked his notes and reminded me of some of the
things I had said during the previous day's psilocybin session.
In particular, he quoted, "I am amazing, and I say that in all
humility." With a flush of embarrassment, yes, I did remember
making that statement, and it was not the way I usually regarded or presented myself. But it wasn't until I was at home
again that I could reconstruct the insight behind it.

During the session I had been lifted to the integrated level
of Self, acknowledging that I was a functioning entity able to
think, act, and connect with its Source. In that expanded state
there was every contrast with my human identity, so concerned
with acceptance and appearances, defensive and yet self-critical.
Teachings I respected would distinguish it as the "I" of pure
awareness compared to the "me" of personality, what Dr.
Griffiths must have meant by ego, and yet this also showed
that the limited "me" is the point of contact with everything
beyond.

I told Matt and Mary that once you know that the Light
composes all of physical matter then walking on water seems

perfectly reasonable. Spontaneous healing could be explained the same way. If everything is being created new each instant, it can be a very small step between being flawed one moment and perfect the next. Even though I felt I had encountered the power that maintains physical reality, I wasn't able to fully comprehend it or to operate from that level, the access we normally think of as performing miracles.

Matt told me that psilocybin is sometimes called a "non-specific amplifier." I loved the term and immediately wrote it down. According to this model, psilocybin brings nothing new in its physical composition, he said, it just opens doors and breaks down barriers, revealing and amplifying the recipient's own beliefs and qualities. He speculated I may have had one of the higher doses this time, because a certain amount would be needed to achieve "escape velocity."

Matt and Mary also said that the entheogen likely demonstrated the level of understanding I have reached over years of spiritual inquiry, and both of them praised me for "doing the work" that made this possible. I replied that although my study was long and sometimes difficult, it was always rewarding and I had been clear about wanting to do it. I regarded the revelations of the previous day as the combined result of preparation and intention, plus a generous dollop of divine grace.

I was delighted — not just to have had that extraordinary experience, but to share it with Mary and Matt. So few friends knew this aspect of me or had an interest in such things that I was grateful to be recognized by these people who were themselves so perceptive. I realized it was my very ego that was getting the positive reinforcement, but I would deal with the implications of that some other time. For the moment, it was a pleasant novelty.

When I met with Dr. Griffiths, he inquired whether I'd had any nausea or headaches the evening before. I told him yes, but they were mild. He was glad to hear that I had been successful this time in following without resistance. I repeated that the first psilocybin session had given me a valuable lesson, a frame of reference, for dealing with the effects of the substance this time.

In many ways, I said, seeing the Light and wanting to remain in that state corresponded to a near-death experience. It was as astonishing and dramatic as I would have thought, and surely my life would never be the same. The memory would remain with me not just as a personal comfort or a promise of all the wonders that I will encounter again, but as a testament to an ongoing mystery in which I am constantly immersed, whether or not I remain aware of it.

If indeed every human experience affects the planet, my encounter with the Light had to have helped elevate the full spectrum of thought and activity, even though it was facilitated by an entheogen. I told Dr. Griffiths that it was also heartening to think that any advances I have made in dealing with fear during the program would serve me usefully in all aspects of my life.

It was fascinating to get a glimpse of that reality, though I saw no way we could function in it as physical beings. I felt sure that even though it might be difficult to hold the vision, one day I would return to that state, and beyond, as my true home.

Until those moments in the Divine Presence I had not fully comprehended the heart of one of the most basic spiritual teachings: the magnificence of the Light not only was there all the time, but continues to operate at every moment — *this* moment. We draw our being from Its substance, new each instant. Its life is our life. It gives everything, asks nothing, and remains constant. I could spend the rest of my days contemplating this one aspect alone.

The energy of this Light is coursing through the universe every second, directing the path of galaxies, the rhythm of oceans, and the impulses that instruct our very cells to perform their work without our conscious knowledge or direction. *"With this as Cause, there can be no mistakes."*

CHAPTER 6

Discovery and Disillusion

My meetings with the staff on the day after the second psilocybin session had been fairly brief, since there were no significant concerns to discuss. I left the Bayview campus in the bright afternoon, still excited, alert, and happy. After driving only about ten minutes I became aware of a flurry of inspirations coming at me wildly. I fumbled for a notebook and pen, trying to scribble them down with no more than a glance to make sure they were landing on the page while I steered the car with one hand and tried to watch the road. The blaze of contact would fade away, then a half-hour or so later some other detail or interpretation would flare up. These cycles would repeat and overlap.

The open gateway was exciting. Some of the thoughts were so distinctly worded that they seemed to qualify as messages, while others were vague impressions or feelings. I had heard about receiving information in this manner, where the recipient assigns appropriate words. It had happened to me only a few times before when I was asking for help, including the response from my body that I had sensed just weeks earlier, after the first dose of psilocybin.

I was aware that I could express many of the images in a variety of ways, and would experiment until each of these seemed accurate. It was like watching a flower bloom. Petals would open. A pause. More petals would unfold. The form began to become more recognizable as a flower instead of a bud, as the manifestation instead of the potential. Being able to interpret the form as words was an added gift, translating symbols into language.

The first message that I received was, *"Now see what flows into your life because you have presented yourself in good faith."* Later came a less-poetic clarification, *"Let's be clear about how this works: I give to you, you pass it on. Got it?"*

Another message sounded like a consolation, *"Once the door is opened, it will never again be completely closed,"* and a little later came the addition, *"as long as you wish it."* Other very personal assurances were given to me as well. This intuitive communication seemed to continue or echo the gentler psilocybin effects in normal life.

During the drive I heard an orchestral version of a familiar Puccini aria on the radio, and it reminded me so much of my tender exchange with the Light that I found myself in tears. I treasured those states and felt the expansion was deeply moving and integrally real, bubbling up from a hidden stream beneath our normal awareness.

A Private Retreat

For several days I was sensitive to heightened perceptions and emotions. Everything seemed more intense, more joyous, more significant, and I felt I had access to exciting new tools to help shape my reality. I even wondered if I'd permanently blasted open some portal to psychic powers, but that slipped away nearly as quickly as it began. A few days later the coach had turned back into a pumpkin and I was left with a lovely memory and a couple of stray sparkles zinging around my brain.

As the phenomenon waned, I often felt a keen sense of loss or separation, which was probably a predictable reaction. I longed for the company of the staff members who had been with me, the only ones I knew who could understand. I tried to coax insights to the surface by writing, but then any account of the event would be reduced only to words, unable to convey the fullness and conviction of the experience itself. Because it was so precisely attuned to me, though, so incommunicable, I could contentedly go about my life knowing a secret.

Listening to particular pieces of music from the sound-track brought back the feelings vividly. Sometimes I would stand in front of the speakers with tears welling up in my eyes, transported again beyond the ordinary. I had learned that my favorite of the ethereal pieces came from the same Brahms *Requiem* as one of the other selections I found threatening. So I'd put on what I called the "high altitude music," the luminous *Selig sind*, and drift back into that beautiful space. The lush, full choral passages contrasting with quiet intervals suggested sunlight and shadow playing across a pastoral landscape. I could almost see what I was hearing.

Three days after the session I had a forehead-smacking realization that I *did* have altered perceptions during the experience. When I'd answered no to the staff's questions, we were all assuming the changes would have been visual. Instead, I had a pronounced reaction to the *music* while the psilocybin was waning in the afternoon. I remembered asking Mary, as I lay on the couch with the eye mask and headphones, "Who could write this? Who could capture this with pen and paper? This isn't a human art; this is channeled from another realm. How can a composer invent this, make this up, transpose this into notes? How can a musician pick up an instrument and make a sound like this? It comes from somewhere else, not this world." It seemed as if the emotions, the power to influence, were embedded within the musical sequence itself, not merely called forth from the listener's imagination. I was sensing the music as an integral whole, more than the sum of its parts, just as I had perceived my amazing Self.

And the more I thought about it, what a strange co-incidence that the supernatural Light was revealed just after my eye mask was removed. Perhaps the light in the room had triggered the opening, at the same time that the physical free-dom of removing the headphones tipped the balance toward joy and release.

For days, I stayed at home and quietly let these matters settle. I talked with a few friends on the phone, but was in no hurry to dilute this private retreat by being out in public.

Every time I looked in the mirror I was surprised to see the same face, the same body that I saw a few days before. How could that be when I was so changed? My visit to higher planes was no less miraculous because it was made possible by an entheogen. Thousands of people throughout history had reached this point, I knew. Some achieved it spontaneously or through discipline and attunement, and others with the aid of hallucinogens. I was merely one voice in the age-old chorus. I was honored to be a part of this society at last. I wanted this. I *asked* for this. I had pushed past my fears and found the courage to come back for the second dose of psilocybin — that had to count for something.

During my years of spiritual inquiry I had been trying to reconcile the traditional concept of a personal God, which I had always accepted, with a broader concept of God that Seth calls a psychic energy gestalt, the sum of all creation and all potential.[11] During the second psilocybin session I tapped into this sense of God as gloriously comprehensive, inexhaustible, and dynamic. I do not claim to have been in the presence of the ultimate Godhead; I doubt I could have returned. Yet on the white couch I also encountered an intensely intimate and loving aspect of the Creator as well, willing to accommodate me in my present state of development. This beautifully illustrated the Sufi teaching that we are a "continuum of consciousness" ranging from the boundless to the personal, and that the spiritual task of awakening is to reconcile and embrace the two.[12]

As my functional personality had fallen away, vaporized into pure essence, the deeper, broader sense of "I am" emerged. It was this core identity that observed and remembered at all levels and enabled me to describe the experience in their shared language.

When I first told Matt and Mary about the primary statement from God and included it in my report, I had written, "Everything is in My perfect control." This had been a direct perception, not delivered in any medium as limiting as words. But later I decided that my phrasing was inaccurate. "Control" brought to mind the dictates of the Old Testament God of might and wrath. A more appropriate translation that would account for God's total awareness and His loving allowance and support of all things would be, "Everything is in My perfect keeping."

It also occurred to me that the second part was curiously

reversed. I understood God's declaration as, "With this as Cause, [you can see that] there can be no mistakes," instead of "With this as Cause, all is perfection." I had to do some careful editing even then to find the best expression. In my first account of the experience I wrote, "With this as direction, there can be no mistakes." Later I decided "With this as Source" was a better interpretation. In the end I chose "With this as Cause" because it added a more accurate sense of will and projection to the concept.

It was interesting, too, to reflect on the exchange where God asked if there were anything I wanted. It occurred to me days later that if I had been able to name anything at all, if I'd had any desire for objects or conditions, it would have been an indication that I was not in the true Presence where all is complete. In that state, I did not inhabit a world of *having*, just *being*, though I was vaguely aware that the other existed elsewhere. As it was, when I said there was nothing I wanted, God could well have winked and said, "Right answer."

Of course, knowing all things, God does not need to ask if there is anything I want. The question, then, becomes more of an invitation to me to redefine myself: "Now that you have this greater understanding, consider yourself within the whole. Look again and tell me whether there is anything you could ever lack."

Comparing that journey with everyday life, I could see how thoroughly our usual state of awareness is defined and limited by our senses. My own identification with my physical body remained during the action of psilocybin. When I felt that wings were being spread over me, for example, I seemed to be looking directly up at them from my same reclining position on the couch. Even in my altered state the assumption of form remained.

Some teachings say that certain abilities and levels of knowledge become available to us naturally as we make spiritual progress. But until we reach those stages organically, such a vision can occur only through a gift of grace, if indeed that is not the only way it can be experienced. At this time I could do no more than stand at the gate, hoping for a glimpse of the Presence of God. Without doubt, the transcendence of the second psilocybin session was a loving gift.

I sensed that keeping the experience vital and maintaining the communication would be mainly up to me. For this, all I would need was to learn to be still, to remember, and to plumb the depths of my psyche to find the secret door again. In time I hoped to establish the path more and more directly, relying on the memory of that mystical experience for guidance. The masters learn to go there unerringly and *live* from there.

After those moments with the Divine, I knew meditation would have a new meaning to me — less of a chore or a discipline and more of an avenue of return. Bartholomew says:

> Meditation, done properly in whatever form it takes, has as its basic function *the conscious absorption of life force into your body* so you can have access to more power, more energy and more awareness…. Meditation is a state where you are constantly recharging the Light within….[13]

What Was He Like?

Two weeks after the session and its follow-up the next day, I returned to Baltimore for another meeting with the staff. We opened with a few quiet moments, then reviewed an augmented report I had written about the recent psilocybin session.

I was still reveling in the joy of the lofty experience, and I had told Mary and Matt about the messages I'd received after my most recent visit to their offices. The staff was happy for me, and seemed to regard that contact as a lingering extension of the state I had reached during the activity of psilocybin.

When Matt inquired about my perception of God during the psilocybin session, I realized my dominant impression was not the single word most often used to characterize the Divine: Love. Matt reminded me that I had described It, rather, as Intelligence. Having been in the Presence on only that one occasion, I told him, I could not be sure that would be the only way I would ever perceive God. These are just two different approaches to a single whole. Intelligence may simply represent the aspect I am attuning to now, or perhaps that God chose to reveal to me.

Other conventional theological descriptions also applied. The Light knows everything because it *is* everything, which made "omniscient" and "omnipresent" redundant. "Omnipotent" seemed an obvious choice, but it suggested the issue of authority that humans insist on attributing to God. Sheer Light has no judgment or reservation, it simply radiates its essence. This constant emanation, this function as ultimate Source, was something that I had read about many times; my acquaintance with the principle helped me recognize that quality.

The press release on Johns Hopkins' first psilocybin study stated that 22 out of 36 volunteers said they had a significant spiritual experience, so my account didn't seem so exceptional. They all had a high dose, Mary noted, and Matt informed me that during the current study, even with multiple doses not all volunteers had such an experience.

As we discussed the arrangements for the recent session, Mary commented that I was still fighting the eye mask and headphones, a criticism which was probably true but smarted all the same because I felt I had made concessions.

I brought the translation from the CD liner notes of the two selections from the Brahms *Requiem*, so at last we'd know what we were listening to. The *Selig sind* was, "Blessed are those who mourn, for they shall be comforted," from Jesus' Sermon on the Mount, and the *Denn alles Fleisch* lyrics translated as, "All flesh is like grass, and the splendor of man is like the flower of the field. The grass dries up, the flower fades and falls to the ground, but the Word of the Lord remains in eternity," a quotation from St. Peter.

We talked about my contention that certain pieces of music sounded "otherworldly" enough to have been drawn from higher levels by the composer. By contrast, several of the selections on the soundtrack seemed to me contrived and pretentious, a tinny human imitation of what glory should sound like. The *Sanctus* that distracted me during the most soaring moments was one of these.

Mary pointed out that a person in a traditional religious practice might regard it as the height of reverence, and she said that some of the volunteers liked it very much. I understood that those volunteers might share the context in which the *Sanctus* was written, within the institutional church. But my perception of Holy (the definition of "sanctus") had changed a great deal from the version I'd been taught. Since I couldn't argue with personal preference, this left me to fret about the fine line between intuition and opinion, or belief and truth.

After the meeting with Matt and Mary, I had the luxury of a half-hour with Dr. Griffiths, though Mary said he would not

be available when I came back the next week to fill out questionnaires. He was open and relaxed as we went over my
report.

Just as Mary had noticed, Dr. Griffiths also thought that I
was fighting against the eye mask and headphones. He cupped
his hands together to show how I was "collapsing the field"
and creating my own limitations. When I proposed that volunteers might discover the Light more easily without the eye
mask, he said that they sometimes tended to lose their focus
and become distracted by the intrusion of waking reality when
the mask and headphones were removed during a session.
Okay, that sounded reasonable — I conceded one more point
for the protocols.

Dr. Griffiths suggested the "dancing" aspect of my experience with the Light, the give-and-take exchange, may have
come from a blurring of my identity as I was partially absorbed
into the Light and then again perceived myself separate from
it. That was a lovely way of looking at it. There had been a
sense that the transitions were almost between me and no-me,
and I was pleased to have this new perspective.

If that were true, I said, maybe I'd been able to shed more
of the ego than I had thought. There was no time and space
where I was, yet because I maintained a continuous awareness,
broader and more secure than my usual definition of self, my
consciousness *included* time and space. And when God asked if
there were anything I wanted and I said no, exactly who was
giving that answer? Maria has many things she wants, and God
surely knows as much. If the "I" who responded was the oversoul, the observer, then where was the everyday definition of
the ego?

Dr. Griffiths seemed to be enjoying the philosophical discussion. He clasped his hands over one knee as he smiled and gazed up at the ceiling to speculate on answers. I was soaking up this thoughtful conversation with a man usually too busy for such indulgences.

"Something as profound as that experience surely has to permanently imprint one's energy field," I said. "If anyone walking down the street could read auras, they would come up to me and say, 'You've seen God, haven't you.' " I expected this to raise his scientific hackles, but he nodded quietly.

And then the day after the session I'd had those insights and messages as I was driving. Dr. Griffiths was willing to credit those as being legitimate, too. All of this supported Huxley's statement that "... the man who comes back through the Door in the Wall will never be quite the same as the man who went out." [14]

I reported that I had recently visited a Tibetan meditation center in Washington, listening to some instructions and sitting with the group for a while. It felt a bit uncomfortable, I said, with all the unfamiliar names and ceremonies, but I told him I was being conscientious about establishing a meditation practice, and thought I might supplement the "empty mind" style of meditation with reading, music, and visualization. He had no objection to that.

As Dr. Griffiths walked me back down the hall to Mary's office, I told him that the spiritual tone seemed as strong as the scientific one at the States of Consciousness Research Project. We briefly discussed the wide availability of spiritual information in many media, and that comparatively few people pursue it, or do so only within "safe" boundaries like religion. Those subjects were always so much more appealing to me than the business of modern society where, Wordsworth wrote, "getting and spending we lay waste our powers." [15]

Mary took me downstairs to sign out, then stepped outside with me to get a breath of fresh air and to talk for a few minutes. I told her, "My life is revolving around this project." It had come to resemble a full-time occupation for me. I said that I had no idea what to expect when my part in the study was over.

"You will find your own circle of friends," she replied. It was meant to reassure me, but all I heard was, "You will be somewhere else — not here, not with us." I couldn't imagine leaving after all we'd been through together, and with practically no one else in my life to talk with about these things. I had to keep in mind that the staff members were being paid to have meetings with me, and they were naturally kind people who would not want to be brusque or rude. It would be futile to try to hold on to the connection in a needy way. I would have to release everyone, most of all myself, from the sharp loss when these people were gone from my life, but at the moment it was unimaginable. I set out for home, turning my attention to happier recent events instead.

About ten days later, I was back in Baltimore for the battery of questionnaires scheduled three weeks after every psilocybin session. As Mary was checking to make sure all the items were completed, she noticed that I had marked off an affirmative answer to whether I considered the recent session with the hallucinogen one of the most meaningful experiences in my life. She and Matt understood the significance of this new response to a question that I had answered differently before. When she verified the information with me, she was beaming.

Our conversation that day was particularly relaxed. There

was nothing stressful to review, and although I had another session scheduled for the following week, obviously my fear was gone. I described a couple of dreams and mentioned a recent conversation with a friend who had advised me to go back to work to maintain some income. Later I had received an inner message that I should tell her, "But I *am* working." Mary and Matt could see my viewpoint and were also amused at the message. Matt added, "And working very hard, too!"

I was pleased to still be receiving messages occasionally, I said. "But I have no idea where they're coming from. Are they from angels or my special guides? From my Higher Self? From God?" Mary counseled that maybe I shouldn't be so quick to distinguish among them, that they were all really the same source. I liked that perspective; it painted the universe as friendly, generous, and cooperative. It also showed me I was happy to get messages from outside and accepted those as credible, but I was dismissing any wisdom of my own.

After we wrapped up our meeting, I went back to Mary's office to answer the final batch of questions at her computer as we talked intermittently. I had not expected to see Dr. Griffiths that day, but he had returned early from his business trip and had a few minutes for me after all. He came to Mary's office for the meeting, the door not-quite-closed again, as Mary left us to a private conversation. I was starting to feel more comfortable in our discussions, and had begun to think of him as "Roland," as Mary and Matt addressed him.

I told him I had been delighted to receive messages, then I worried because some teachers say they're just for you and they shouldn't be revealed until you are better grounded. Roland commented that, yes, this was good advice, but mainly one should be careful about operating from ego, seeking praise and validation. That was the way I had always understood "ego," so it was easy to see his point.

Roland went on to caution me not to be overconfident about the upcoming sessions. Just because I had moved beyond some personal boundaries and had a transcendental experience, he said, I must not assume there is nothing more to learn. Instead I should welcome the opportunities that remain and continue to approach them with humility. He always offered succinct and cogent advice, and I listened carefully.

I knew he was correct, but I stated with certainty that the impact of the initial encounter with psilocybin could never again shock me, and any such challenges would be much less likely to derail me in the future. At least I had that learning curve in my favor. He agreed. I realized the process could still be deep and confrontational, I explained, and I was resolved to work with whatever occurred. I also intended to rehearse the two Brahms pieces again and to put myself in a frame of mind to face psychological demons if that were required.

A Troubling New Perspective

My third psilocybin session was exactly a week away, and I was looking forward to it. The research project was nearly the only thing on my mind during that time. On Tuesday night, two days before the session, I went online to review again the press release about the institution's first study on psilocybin. This time I followed the links to information about Roland and to a question-and-answer interview, and then on to professional commentaries on that study.

Roland's résumé was impressive: pages of academic degrees and credentials, certifications, honors, awards, professional memberships, journal editor and reviewer positions, his national, international, and industry consultant activities, and collaboration on hundreds of articles. His special interests in caffeine and benzodiazepines, I learned, included studies conducted with both animals and humans. "Research with baboons and rats involves drug discrimination, physical dependence, tolerance, schedule-controlled behavior, drug self-administration, and drug administration to discrete brain sites. ... These studies will provide information about behavioral and pharmacological mechanisms of action and neuroanatomical sites of action of these widely prescribed therapeutic agents."

In the written interview, Roland presented a persuasive case for this and future research on hallucinogenic drugs. He spoke eloquently of the prospects for using psilocybin therapeutically, carefully distinguishing current methods from the drug experiments of the 1960s. [Appendix II]

By the time I got to the commentaries on the first psilocybin study at Johns Hopkins, the approach had become noticeably more clinical. Four research professionals in the field praised the rigor of the study's design and execution, its careful accounting for set and setting, and the preparation of the volunteers. But from there they spun off into details about comparable drugs, methods, and criteria of measurement. One stated that psychedelics "act primarily by activating serotonin 5-HT_{2A} receptors, especially those densely expressed on the apical dendrites of cortical pyramidal cells." Another had written that, "It is clear that the effects of psilocybin were more than expectancy effects because the active drug control condition (30 mg of methylphenidate) did not produce similar effects on ratings of significance or on measures of spirituality, positive attitude, or behavior." They agreed that psilocybin had the potential to produce an extraordinary experience, and that its study could "help us understand molecular alterations in the brain that underlie mystical religious experiences." The authors cited the high incidence of such experiences in the volunteers and their enhanced outlooks and moods in follow-up interviews. Roland was widely praised for the design and execution of this study and his overall contributions to the field.

Ordinarily I would have regarded such accomplishments as admirable and trust-inspiring, but that evening the circular references and the cumulative weight of the jargon began to sound like so much self-congratulation. I was abruptly reminded that the more spiritual-minded Roland I had come to know was no less a dispassionate, dedicated and focused man of science.

As I read on, a troubling new perspective began to emerge. The emphasis was on the data the researchers had gathered, while the role of those of us serving anonymously in the trenches seemed incidental. The approach even appeared to favor the accumulation of data over establishing a reliable route of access to the Divine itself. Despite my marvelous experience in the second session and all the support and care I'd received, from this point of view my function as a volunteer seemed to be nothing more than a lab rat. I felt manipulated, deceived, and just plain used. I was embarrassed and angry to think I had walked right into the setup, performed predictably, and delivered exactly the results they were expecting. My reports of luminous expansion and the very private reflections I had confided to the staff just seemed to play into their hands.

Participating in this study had been the most remarkable thing that had ever happened to me, and now I was facing the fact that my response was merely standard; the staff had heard it all before. I was one more computer entry, another page of checkmarks to tally. My personal growth seemed irrelevant. I was just a number to them.

That evening I had also come across the Consent Form I had signed, and noticed the words, "This study is not designed or intended to provide any direct benefits to you." In the light of all I had just discovered, the disclaimer seemed like unforgivable arrogance, which only increased my resentment, though I had read it before and was happy at the time to join the study.

That simple, straightforward background on the project broadsided me more strongly than perhaps it should have. I couldn't attribute my reaction to any other causes at the time. If I was honestly seeking information when I read those online reports, I had to be willing to accept it and to acknowledge my limited role in the project. After all, I thought, it's not as if they ever pretended to be doing anything except research. And I had indeed experienced the best of what they promoted for that entheogen.

It was well after midnight when I went to bed, after trying to blow off steam by writing in my journals. The next day my disappointment and sense of betrayal remained strong. There just wasn't enough time to make peace with the whole episode. I could see I was going to be carrying over the feelings to my next session, now only a few hours away.

CHAPTER 7

Not Knowing Is an Art

My brother Lance had agreed to drive me to Baltimore for the third session. I packed an overnight bag and left the house before dawn, drove forty miles to Lance's, and was that much closer to Baltimore. I was grateful that my brother and sisters would sacrifice a whole day for my interests.

We arrived on time and Lance dropped me at the door. I brought a pillow and an art book, and was still optimistic enough to pack a lunch, though I hadn't been able to eat yet on a session day. Ben, the program assistant I'd met before, brought me upstairs and sent the urine sample to the lab. No one was assuming anything about that, either. I heard Roland asking him whether it checked out all right.

While the interior room was being set up, Roland met with me in Mary's office for a brief conversation which began routinely. I was nervous, however, about possibly sabotaging the session. The staff had reminded me several times that volunteers could experience paranoia during the activity of psilocybin, and since so many negative feelings remained from my readings about the project, I seemed poised to do just that.

I had no idea how these misgivings might surface. What if

I fell into a sulk and undermined the whole day's program? What if I blasted these people with some unexpected rant? Better safe than sorry, I thought, so I confessed to Roland that about 36 hours earlier I had become disillusioned with the project when I came upon the dry, scientific reports online. Instead of being appreciated for my role, I complained, now I could see I was just a number to them, a set of data. I felt like a lab rat subjected to arbitrary conditions while they formulated theories in an ivory tower.

As this spilled out, I apologized and told Roland I realized it was an overreaction and in no way reflected the kindness of the staff. I had tried to work through the problem on my own, I said, but I thought I should mention this personal sting in case something relevant surfaced during the session. (This was also a convenient excuse to let them know I was on to them, even if the issue didn't come up.)

Roland brightened when I told him this and said that my admission was a valuable contribution. He spent a few minutes assuring me that the staff and fellow researchers were not all ogres, and that the academic tone was a reflection of the necessary methodology, then dashed off to inform Matt and Mary of this development. I could see Roland's eyes twinkle as if one of his four-footed rats had escaped from its cage and left an irreverent note.

In the session room, Mary and Matt wanted to be sure my concerns were addressed before we proceeded. Considering the project from the different perspective I found online, they said, it was understandable that I could interpret the information as I did. I explained that my peeve was not directed at either of them, and that I was still committed to participating in the study.

Without further distraction we turned our attention to the day's business. The couch was made up with sheets and blanket, and a red rose and bowl of grapes were set out again. Matt took a baseline blood pressure reading as I listened to the music track, then Roland joined us.

I settled into those surroundings that now I could associate with my recent mystical experience. In some way I felt as if I had already taken the dose, I told the staff. If not an actual altered state, the memory of it had welled up in me. There was the same rush of fear, the same trepidation about the power of the entheogen I was about to face. I had built a degree of trust in the process by now and could anticipate how the music would direct my day, but a well-earned respect remained, as if I were setting out to cross the ocean in a rowboat. I suggested this reaction might be the result of my intention, and was pleased when Roland agreed, since he had advised me the previous week to prepare with humility and be careful of over-confidence. And yes, I was glad to be back on the white couch, for better or worse. We held an impromptu little ceremony, and I swallowed the capsule offered in the brown goblet.

Roland took his leave, and I sat quietly with my two guides to look at the art book I'd brought. In about twenty minutes I began to suspect that I had taken an active dose; its onset was gradual and tolerable.

We all knew the procedure and were efficient at putting on the eye mask, headphones and blood pressure cuff. The feelings of sinking and disorientation returned, but they were not as intense as before, so I thought I had received a lesser dose. I felt some of the spicy-hot radiation in my face at the onset, and similar sensations in my stomach and abdomen as the substance worked its way through my system. The physical surges returned, too, but by this point they were of little concern. I knew they were harmless and would subside, and I had become accustomed to them in my normal state anyway. As the full effect of the psilocybin took hold, I became oriented to the alternate reality.

From time to time there would be a new "bloom" of depth, even after I was already submerged. Now there was a familiarity to this inner space, and I found I was able to navigate much more easily than during the previous sessions. I felt no fear and was able to keep an even keel emotionally and psychologically, and to largely maintain the role of observer. I told Mary it was like learning to ride a bicycle and leaning into the turns.

Once again, there was only blackness in this dimension, no hallucinations or images. My mind and all my senses were operating normally except my restricted sense of sight, and I missed it very much. A view of the room without the eye mask would have been no use at all. It was information on the unknown other world that I longed for.

Because I was revisiting a consistent and convincing plane, which I knew contained wonders ranging from the cellular level to the Divine Light itself, I didn't understand why so much of it was hidden from me. Still, I was relieved to find it somewhat as it had seemed before. I had no feelings of being inebriated, although at times my mind was not focused in my waking self. In the greatest depths I often found myself thinking quite clearly in normal patterns, yet willing to surrender to whatever else might arise.

I asked Matt and Mary to write down a few things for me so that I would remember, because the impressions flickered away and I would move on. Especially in the early stages, speaking was difficult or impossible. At other times I fairly forced myself to describe my perceptions aloud so that there would be some record.

Visit to a Dark Land

On this journey I was accompanied by silent and invisible guardians and watched by those who ruled the realm. Rather than a single Power presiding, I sensed there were multiple beings. Early in my immersion several of the guides in that reality made a quick check on the mysterious "program" I felt I had received in my body during the session a month earlier. As they drew back a covering I glimpsed what resembled a beautiful pink enameled egg with bands of diamonds. The guides established that all was well and covered it again. (Reflecting on this a few days later, I considered how unlikely it was to come upon this reference. It provided a validation to that strange event, which still defied interpretation.)

Soon after that I told Mary I found myself at a place I had forgotten from the second session where a large door was set high up on an inaccessible cliff. I had been told that the door would not be opened to me at that time. Now there was no door and no message, but somehow I knew I was at the same landmark, which was unaccountable in a dark land with no way to judge depth or distance. Later I guessed that, instead of being visual, my cue may have been the piece of music at that point on the soundtrack.

Once I reached a certain depth I felt sure that I was in the area where the Light had appeared previously. I yearned to see It, but had no way of finding It. I thought perhaps It had not returned because of my misinterpretation or inadequacy, but I remembered the caution about being distracted by subjective judgment. Instead I stayed alert and hoped maybe there was still a chance the Light would reveal Itself. Each time I noticed Its absence, I was disappointed but carefully redirected my attention.

There were times I felt tenderly watched over. I told Mary and Matt that I was embraced from behind so that I knew who was there even though I was not able to see. It was the Divine, supporting and loving but not visible. Another time I felt a long cord going out from my identity in this altered state to the self in waking consciousness, like a spacewalking astronaut on a lifeline, and knew that sustaining love is being sent to our physical counterpart constantly through this connection. Even when we totally forget our source, I said, we are nevertheless dearly loved, and the realization brought me to tears.

Now adjusting more comfortably to this reality, there was greater ease in reaching and maintaining a more profound level of "letting go." There were periods when Nothing (capital N) was happening, and I was content with that. I was aware of being in a void, though I could not be sure whether it was "The Void" of legend, where I rested in peace and content-ment for some time. Easing out of one of those occasions enough to articulate an insight, I asked Matt to write down my words because it seemed so important: "Not Knowing is an art." That is, "Not Knowing" as a suspension of labeling reality, an acceptance of undefined conditions, and the relinquishing of personal control, rather than "Not Knowing" as ignorance. As I understood it from my reading, this non-form is a state or function of the void or potential. It is the "stem cell" of mani-festation; it can become anything.

(At the end of the day I remembered this one significant statement as, "Not Knowing is a gift." After Matt checked his notes and said I had called it an *art*, I saw even more subtlety in the phrase. That would suggest it can be cultivated rather than bestowed, and that it could have nuances. I was finally beginning to develop some tolerance for ambiguity.)

Still hoping to find the Light, I asked the unseen beings, "Where is God?" They did not answer directly, but inquired nonverbally whether I would like to practice being a creator myself. They offered me a wand or baton and invited me to step up on a podium like an orchestra conductor, but I was embarrassed and declined. A short time later they encouraged me to try again, and once more I was flustered and had no idea where to begin. However I thought it would be useful to practice the exercise when I returned to my waking state because some teachers say we are constantly creating anyway and must learn to do it consciously. This was a good lesson. It was also an appropriate answer to my question.

As in my first psilocybin session, many of my perceptions were expressed in the imagery of water. On that occasion I had been tumbled over rapids and churned under waves. This time the waters were much more placid. I felt as if I were drifting through the darkness in a small craft, observing and being observed. I was carrying my own banner and making a statement simply by standing alone.

My boat explored a number of bays and eddies as my travels continued, but there was no one to greet me and nothing to see. Somehow it seemed that each of the areas was distinctive, even though I was not sure why I was guided there. I told Mary and Matt that my cells would remember and be imprinted with the knowledge of those places, like a stamp on a passport. After the session, I thought perhaps the areas had been differentiated by the sequence of the music selections.

But progress in this strange landscape was slowing. I had found nothing to characterize the journey as dramatically as the vision of the Light which occurred in the second session, so I worried that I was letting down the staff.

I felt an accountability and a debt of gratitude to those who'd sponsored my voyage to inner space, even though they were content to be getting their information from questionnaires and hadn't asked for postcards or souvenirs. The program's architects knew I would be having nearly indescribable adventures in another realm, learning my way around completely unfamiliar territory. My body was safe on the white couch, but my mind was keenly aware of being projected far beyond the ordinary. I regretted that I could not fully communicate this experience to Matt and Mary and I complained to them, "What use is it to anyone if you can't be here with me? How can I possibly convey enough to make this worth your while?"

I had never been clear about what was expected of the volunteers. Perhaps we were screened for some ability to perceive spiritual revelations or formulate original insights when exposed to universal truths or to interpret obscure realms of consciousness with the illumination of psilocybin. Maybe our responses to those 700 questions were being used to define some emerging theological consensus. Or could my answers reveal I'd gone to the wrong place?

Finally I concluded that the researchers were not judging me by my observations or depending on me to document anything in particular. They did not appear to be concerned with the crags and craters of personal mental geography in these altered worlds so much as calculating the right amount of rocket fuel for a targeted landing.

As Big as the Planet

I was still unacquainted with the rules of the reality where I found myself, but I wanted to explore and to show good faith toward the other presences. So I set out to find some task to perform there in the darkness, some contribution I could make beyond reporting what I encountered. I knew how to take action and be creative when grounded in three dimensions, but in these impossibly different conditions, how could I learn more or be helpful or repay the privilege of being allowed to visit?

Not knowing what else to do, I quietly and humbly presented myself to the unseen rulers and said, "Here I am. This is what I have become, and this is what I have to offer you in service." And while I waited in the stillness for some response, it occurred to me that I also could act as an ambassador for others.

Mary and Matt would have marveled at the power of this place too, I was sure. *Anyone* would be amazed if they could visit that world, from which the entire physical universe seemed to originate. I realized that there was no one on earth who did not draw their being from there, so I stood as a representative for all.

As I connected with the level where we are united, I omitted the layer of personalities and conflicts and spoke for only the truest, most basic characteristics that define us. I felt as if I were at the prow of a great ship moving through dark waters with all of mankind following in my wake, and I described this to Matt and Mary.

And then an even greater expansion opened to me. Besides humanity, I found trees and rocks coming into my scope, and I included them as well. The entire planet was within my purview, so I brought it too in homage and humility. I was not being elevated by popular acclaim, no one was aware of this, but as a participant in the earth's physical expression I could serve as an exemplar with full ownership and authority. So I stood in the dark before I-knew-not-whom and declared allegiance for all of us, united in our perceptions and development, to those mentors and guardians. After a long and peaceful silence I received a quiet but significant nod of recognition from the Powers, and the mission was done. No trumpets, no choirs, no words or images.

(Days later I remembered that Rudolf Steiner describes the Archangel Michael as silent and reserved,[16] so I wondered if it had been Michael before whom I stood. I have a great admiration for Michael, and admire his esoteric reputation. Steiner calls him "the fiery Cosmic Lord of Thought," [17] and says he is the Time Spirit of our age.[18])

Later in the session I felt like my body was a bridge across which information or blessing was being conveyed back to the planes of earth. There was no glory or distinction for me because of this, it was just a function of being part of the whole.

Although I was moved by the music soundtrack during my session the previous month, this time I attuned to it even more closely. Its beautiful mid-day selections were perfectly timed to the arc of the psilocybin's effect on the body. During its height, I seemed to be gliding effortlessly like a wide-winged bird on an updraft. This prolonged state was the crest of the entire experience. When the sweetness was interrupted by a soprano, I said, "Mary, I hope that change in the music is not a signal that I'm supposed to be coming down, because I am nowhere near ready." She assured me all was well and I could continue.

During one particularly lovely piano piece, I asked Mary to make a note of the name of the work for me but added, "Don't tell me now, because I don't want it to have a name. I like it just the way it is." As I had found the previous time, there was a sense that the music was "channeled" from another dimension.

When at last it became evident that the strength of the psilocybin was waning, I was sad to relinquish the access to this other level. My return to the reality of the white couch was slow, steady, and calm, and my airship made a perfect three-point landing.

While I was drifting in the final gentle stages, the multi-part themes of one piece of baroque choral music set off images of elaborate architectural forms building up-up-up like cumulus clouds. I just watched joyfully. And yet, there was nothing to see. I never had any true visual hallucinations — not objects, patterns, colors or lights. I perceived only the kind of thing one would see if asked, say, to imagine an apple: you call to mind a general approximation of what it looks like, but no actual picture floats in front of you. This sort of imagery was all I ever experienced during the action of psilocybin.

At one point late in the session it seemed as if my entire torso had disappeared. I knew I had a head because I could talk, and I knew I had feet because they were cold (and I was too embarrassed to ask Mary for anything so menial as to cover them with the blanket), but I could not detect anything in between except an expanse of emptiness. *Not* feeling my body when I deliberately turned my attention to it was strangely and subtly different than the normal state of not being *aware* of feeling my body unless there was some particular discomfort. I hoped it was enjoying the vacation.

I noticed that the craving for fresh air, cold water, and outdoor spaces did not return as it had in the previous sessions. Perhaps my body had already "learned" psilocybin and felt no need for compensation, or the dose may have been less demanding physically.

An Appreciation of Matt and Mary

Slowly the higher planes receded and my attention returned to the world from which I'd started. I was still reclining on the couch, and would have been dizzy if I had tried to sit up. I was content to leave the eye mask in place rather than deal with too much sensory input. At that time I became more aware of my two excellent supporters, Mary and Matt, and wanted to tell them the details of my experiences. I had established a rapport with Mary during our extra time when I filled out questionnaires, but I did not yet feel I was on the same terms with Matt.

"Are you there, Matt?" I called. "Come talk to me." In only a moment I felt him take my hand. "I want to thank you for everything you do for me. You're always attentive and I never show my appreciation, but I am so grateful. You monitor the equipment and write up the details, and I never acknowledge you. The project is fortunate to have you, and you are lucky to be involved in something like this, too — so young, yet you have your degree and are getting established in this outstanding work. How perceptive you are and what a bright future you have."

This caught Matt a little off guard, but he did not appear to be sidetracked by the praise. Instead he asked, "Isn't there someone else you're forgetting?" No, that someone was just as vital to the project, and just as close to me.

However her formal role might be described, Mary brought a very different sensibility to the project than Matt and Roland. She was the initial point of contact for volunteers, and remained their closest representative and confidante.

"Mary is the glue that holds the project together," I said. "Her nurturing instincts provide the balance to the scientific approach. Mary is our Quan Yin, the heart of the program, and we all depend on her. She constantly impresses me with the breadth of her spiritual references. It's easy to see she's been at this for a long time. Dr. Richards knew what he was doing when he invited Mary to join the staff in this research department."

By this time, Mary was sitting beside me too, all three of us holding hands. I told them I would have loved to have taken them into the experience with me but didn't know how. Mary said that they were aware of its power, which was gradually diminishing. I was happy to have their friendship, which went beyond a job description or an assignment. We talked quietly, absorbed in a loving and peaceful glow. Perhaps such occasions were more familiar to Mary and Matt in their work with the volunteers, but it was very rare for me.

There was another insight that I wanted to bring up, too. "You know how they say that we ourselves determine each event, but usually not consciously? For example, when your life's work is completed and you feel it's time to leave, any method will do. You could be in an auto accident or slip in the bathtub or get hit by a meteorite. It doesn't matter, you don't care, you just need an exit. Well, I must have brought this program into my life in the same way. I had decided to retire this year partly because I wanted more time to devote to my spiritual studies. My Higher Self must have put out the call for a leap in consciousness, and it had to arrive by some method. It could have come from meeting a guru or having a vision or being struck by lightning, but instead it came from an even more unlikely source: I answered an ad for the States of Consciousness project and I took a hallucinogen."

Matt cleverly asked, "So you're saying that you decided to conduct a study and Johns Hopkins volunteered?"

"Exactly!" I replied, and we all laughed. Turning the tables seemed a humorous way to describe the situation, but as far as I was concerned it was absolutely valid.

This intimate exchange with Matt and Mary was just as meaningful to me as the altered reality from which I was returning. Although the connection was obviously still strongly influenced by the effects of psilocybin, it was equally grounded in waking consciousness and drew from a very practical blending of states, the best of both worlds. I had no way of judging how my impressions may have been enhanced, but the staff had always maintained that the feelings originated solely within me.

After a while I was able to open my eyes, sit up and drink some water, and talk more with Matt and Mary. But it was too early to dispense with the protocols, so after a break they had me lie down again with the headphones and eye mask. From time to time our conversation continued.

I told them, "I asked to expand because Bartholomew says, 'If you don't ask, nothing will happen.' [19] I have heard before that the upper realms are not allowed to interfere unless we invite them."

Then a more popular use occurred to me and I said, "Matt, isn't there something like that on Star Trek? Doesn't the crew need a special request before they can intervene?"

"The Prime Directive," he shot back.

I was tickled and said, "I knew you'd know."

When at last I was released from the confinements of the eye mask, headphones, and blood pressure cuff at the end of the session, I freshened up in the bathroom and ate some grapes before I faced the questionnaires. My guess was that I'd had the medium dose of psilocybin that day, so only one more dose was available.

Roland joined us and pulled up a chair to review the day's events. He asked whether I had any fear and I confidently replied no, that I had proceeded with relative ease this time. The session was deep and it had gone smoothly. I added that I had not seen the Light again, but had gone into darkness like a void and sent back the message, "Not Knowing is an art." When I said not much else had happened, Mary interrupted, rolling her eyes. "Oh, right, not much happened! She only expanded her consciousness to include everyone on the earth and the planet itself!" She and Matt chimed in with a more colorful version of the session, and I was glad to hear they had found it significant. At that point I was more intent on remembering my earlier insight about Not Knowing; the planetary expansion was an event completed and done.

In a little while, Lance was brought in to join us. I introduced him as my psychically sensitive organic-farmer brother, and in his trademark denim vest and jeans he looked convincing. The staff was always cordial to my family, and after this visit they advised Lance that I might need some help during the rest of the evening. He and I stopped for dinner on the way home, arriving late and tired.

The next day I drove back to Baltimore happily with my required report. In our meeting that afternoon, I was a little surprised to learn how much Mary and Matt had been affected by our "bonding experience" when I was transitioning from the higher levels on the previous day.

Mary told me that she and Matt and Roland had remained in the room for some time after Lance and I left, talking about the intensity of the session and the personal connections. She seemed pleased by my acknowledgement of her work, and said that Matt, too, had been moved by my praise. But more important to me, she said that both of them could feel my expansiveness and the kinship I was trying to express. Apparently it had been strong enough to be perceptible even to others, but all I could be sure of was how natural and sincere it had been for me. I was sorry Roland could not have been with us too, both to participate in the joy of the moment and to assess it with his own sensibilities and professional criteria.

My lesson for this session may have been just another approach to dealing with reality. Instead of joining the Light, perhaps I was learning to rest in the void. Despite Bartholomew's explanations, I did not yet understand the relationship of the void to the Light, and was not clear on the distinction between "awareness" and "conscious awareness" that he described.[20] There was much to learn.

Amplified Emotions

My initial encounter with psilocybin had been so devastating that it required both a physical recovery and an extended psychological adjustment, and the second was so mystical that I would cherish it for the rest of my life. But even after what I believed to be a lower dose this time, I found myself grappling with the impact a week later. I wished I could have more of those friendly exchanges with the staff, and had to resist impulses to phone them every ten minutes and create a nuisance.

The sense of openness and the emotional intensity were palpable, and I instinctively knew that in order to preserve this condition and to work within it I must be quiet and avoid distraction. This was not constant, but it remained near the surface, always close to breaking though. I tried to think of ways to maintain or recapture the state, but remembered the traditional wisdom that such an ability would require many years of discipline.

By nature I thrive on quiet surroundings and unstructured time, and have taken care to build these into my life. But after this experience I felt an even more intense need to insulate myself while the chrysalis formed. I knew from the previous sessions that this would fade in a few days, which would release me from the vulnerability, but I still wanted to be able to tap its rich depths.

My emotions were often delicately balanced and could teeter one way or the other with little provocation. Whatever I turned my attention to was magnified, for better or worse, though the higher and finer sentiments came more readily. An evocative piece of music would bring a flood of tears, a longing to return to the communion of my altered state, like a flower torn from its roots. I could be open and radiant, yet almost concurrently also seem inadequate and frustrated at my limitations. Feelings of love and compassion alternated with sadness, loss, and inability to communicate this to anyone. Here was a practical example of psilocybin as a "non-specific amplifier." Once the substance opens the door, it is open to everything without discrimination — an exquisite sensitivity to pleasure, pain, and whatever lies in between — and it becomes the task of the individual to sort these through and make peace with them. Being grounded and supported is invaluable, but the work itself remains.

If my reaction was characteristic, then the researchers should recommend that a psilocybin session be followed by a week's retreat. Except for my "baptism by fire" in the first session, everything on the journey warranted further reflection and integration, and I needed time to assimilate it. I could also understand why the study's administrators had asked for volunteers with a background in spirituality. It was the natural key to interpreting these experiences and giving them perspective.

Over a week later I remained homesick and lovesick for that elevated state. It is not the content of the blue capsule that is addictive, I told Mary, but any openness to the Presence of God. I could truly appreciate how the use of psilocybin could be considered a sacrament. The vast potential called me back to explore these dimensions so far beyond human concepts that I could discern little more than darkness. Where else might I be taken and what more could I learn in other voyages?

During the Christmas holidays I enjoyed social events with family and friends, and was even able to do some work in the yard in mild weather. I also went to see an exhibit at the Library of Congress on the production of a new Bible commissioned by St. John's Abbey in Minnesota, using historic methods and materials. I admired the finished pages on display and watched the video showing the parchment being prepared, calligraphers hand-lettering the text and applying gold leaf, and artists designing the book's distinctive original illustration. I deeply identified with the artistic process but felt an uneasy concern that recopying an ancient document seemed misguided when God is speaking to us afresh every moment. The workmanship on the new Bible was gorgeous, and the words still provide lessons and inspiration. But the project perpetuates the belief that this is the single and definitive revelation, when I was more certain than ever that the message is evolving and being revitalized continually.

Stronger

My next meeting with the research team was for the third-week questionnaires early in January. It had been a full year since I had first noticed the ad for the study and had phoned the once-anonymous Mary to introduce myself. I was glad to see her again, but I learned that Matt was out that day so I wouldn't be able to visit with him.

I had sent the staff some excerpts from Seth on massive doses of LSD and personality annihilation.[21] The information was appropriate for Matt in particular. Roland would benefit from reading it too, I thought, but I was not bold enough to suggest any such thing.

While talking with Mary that morning, I mentioned that Roland appeared disappointed that I had not been meditating before I joined the program, noting that other volunteers had much more practice. "But you couldn't have had the experience you did in the second session without a lifetime of spiritual background," Mary said. That was a compliment I treasured, even though I had no way to determine whether it was true. She also commended me for my firm intention to integrate all this into my life.

Just before I began the questionnaires, Mary learned that Roland was leaving the office and would have only a few minutes to meet with me at that time. He came up the hall to Mary's office and she left us alone, with the door ajar as always, for a private talk. He asked about my life in general and how I regarded the most recent session. I told him that I had "gone to the same place" as on previous occasions, which made me wonder what kind of reality I was in. I was feeling more at ease there, I said, and the day had proceeded relatively smoothly. I added that it would seem natural to take psilocybin regularly as a religious practice. He countered by reminding me that similar experiences could be reached by other means. Hallucinogens are simply instruments useful in glimpsing these states, which we can then learn to access directly. Roland quoted the advice of Alan Watts, "When you get the message, hang up the phone." [22]

I told him that I loved the feeling of being expanded so much that I would like to stay that way all the time. I didn't want to let it fade, even though I could easily spend half the time crying. "It won't go," he said. But I did not share his confidence, remembering how the state had waned after previous sessions. The unspoken part of his reassurance was, at the very least, "You won't lose it if you make an effort to maintain it and if you meditate." As Roland opened the door to leave, I realized how much more I wanted to talk with him, but a moment later he was heading back down the hall.

I worked my way through the stack of questionnaires and the computer questions, sometimes talking with Mary. If I had to choose any one word to describe the change I felt in myself over the last year, I told her, it would be "stronger." She agreed with the assessment.

"Now how can you tell that in the short time you've known me?" I asked.

"How could you say all those things about me during your last session in the short time you've known me?" she retorted.

It was already dark, and time for each of us to be getting on our way. As we parted, I added that I was looking forward to the upcoming fourth session on Tuesday. "I hope we've been wrong all this time about what doses I've taken, and at last I get the high dose."

"Just listen to you!" Mary said. "Did you ever think you'd be talking like that after your first session?"

Over the next few days, I happily reviewed the principles that I have infinite resources and can develop the ability to consciously create. "There is joy in having so much to learn and in seeing progress on the path," I wrote in my journals. "How can I help but come out of this stronger?"

But soon enough the poles shifted again, and my confidence was wavering. I was frustrated at not being able to stay connected to that higher level of consciousness. My everyday life seemed pale and unsatisfying after all that spiritual sandblasting. If I were more advanced, I thought, I could have maintained that vision. I felt as if I should get down on my knees to the staff and confess, "I don't know a thing about spirituality. I am a fraud, a charlatan. I somehow managed to fool you all. I know *nothing!* There is God and there is ignorance, and no other alternatives. And I am ignorant, because obviously if I knew anything about God, I would be there in His Presence instead of marooned here in what appears to be a place far, far away." That problematic sense of separation was back again, when I knew that there was no such thing. But I was still immersed in the appearance of physical reality, and not dealing with it well at the moment either.

The prospect of being deprived of the personal expansion *and* my association with the research project was just too much. I wanted to sit and cry. I recognized this as the reverse of the strength-and-radiance mindset. It was probably just the return swing of the pendulum, slowly coming back into balance, but that was insufficient consolation.

And then I put on the Brahms *Requiem* that opened with the *Selig sind* I had come to associate with the mystical state. All my mental contrivances fell away and I was lifted again toward the realms where there is no concern about what the mind should be asking or trying to remember. Only the feeling, the experience itself, remained.

CHAPTER 8

150% of Me

Five days after meeting with the staff for the questionnaires, I had an appointment for my fourth session. I drove to Alida's new home, only ten miles away, and we set off for Baltimore. Once again she had been willing to sacrifice a day of vacation to take me to the appointment. Two sessions remained, and one dose of psilocybin. I felt capable and would have welcomed it that day, but then only the placebo would remain for my last appointment.

I signed in at the desk and was taken upstairs for the usual procedures before a session. While Mary and Matt were setting up the room, Roland gave me his customary preflight briefing in Mary's office. He commented that I appeared to be making good use of the experiences and working diligently with my insights, as the researchers had intended.

Since the subject had been on my mind, I used this occasion to ask about his own involvement with the substance. I said that I had read his statement in an online interview that he had not taken psilocybin. I wasn't trying to elicit an admission that he had, I told him, and I was careful not to use a confrontational tone. "But how can you ask others to do something you haven't done, and why wouldn't you try it if you have any scientific curiosity?"

He paused a moment, seeming to refocus himself at a distance, then spoke quietly and deliberately. It was his *dharma*, he said, to conduct the study in the best interest of science to support the growth of knowledge on the subject, and to do this he needed to remove himself from it and stand as an observer. He said he did not want to influence the study with his personal point of view, nor could he risk subjecting the study to criticism because he had compromised the methodology.

Roland's forthright explanation was consistent with all the careful protocols and standards that characterized the project, and suddenly seemed embarrassingly obvious to me. I had no idea whether he would have wanted to take the entheogen at all, yet I saw obvious advantages if he could experience its effects for himself, and better appreciate what the volunteers were going through.

A few minutes later he joined Matt, Mary and me in the session room, and I took my seat in the center of the white couch once again. Everything was in order for another journey — the four of us, the rose and the bowl of grapes. I knew I was in excellent care, and felt excited about the opportunity to explore. Then suddenly the last-minute shock hit me as it had before the previous sessions. That blue capsule was potent medicine. The staff gently reminded (and teased) that I could still change my mind and decline to take it, but we all knew there was no way I would consider missing the ride.

After I swallowed the dose with the full glass of water, I asked to read a short essay I had prepared for the occasion. In "Three Stories of Learning" I described how I was able to interpret a piece of sheet music for my piano lessons in middle school after hearing an old 78 rpm recording, and I told about being overwhelmed with challenge at the start of a whitewater raft trip only to feel a joyful sense of mastery by the end of the day. My sessions at Johns Hopkins were my third example of learning, drawing from both of these — experiencing things previously known only intellectually, and having such a marvelous adventure that I didn't want to give it up. The staff thanked me graciously, then tucked the paper into my file.

This time the effects began more quickly. The descent was a little unpleasant but not frightening. Once I had stabilized I found myself distracted with thought and judgment for a long time, comparing these alterations with normal consciousness. "This seems to be a viable dose, so next time will be the placebo. This is my last chance for expansion and transcendence. How can I make it count? Is it going to get any deeper?" Because the mind was so busy with analysis, I had difficulty relaxing into the very state I had been anticipating.

At times throughout the day I was disappointed to find that many of my experiences had ceased to be a revelation. While still a remarkable diversion from everyday life, I noticed similarities to former sessions rather than making discoveries. This was particularly true of the music. "Beginner's mind" was gone. I found myself gauging my mental state to what seemed appropriate on the soundtrack, keying it to a series of musical cues. "Oh no, are we up to the Wagner already?"

By the time I was able to let go and work with what I was given, the experience was nearly at its peak. Thankfully, the arc of the entheogen's effects has its own process and duration, so I could slip into the stream again and become immersed in its flow. This was a familiar alternate world, just a little less intense than when I had taken psilocybin before. There were no callings from on high during this session, no visions or visitations. Almost everything was distilled to emotion. I told Mary the most important contribution I was making for the day was just "feeling."

The Power of Emotion

There was only one notable highlight, when I seemed to find myself on a level where I was holding up the world. "If this world continues from moment to moment," I told Matt and Mary, "you have me to thank. Someone else may be taking care of it another time, but for now, it's me."

It took some reflection a few days later for me to reconstruct that scenario. During the experience I had come to see that "feeling," some expansive version of what we would call emotion, was maintaining the physical world. Because of my thorough immersion in it, I sensed that my consciousness was aligned enough to sustain everything in its scope, or that I was operating in a realm where others of the same power held the world in manifestation. The state did not last for very long, nor did it seem like a display of ego, but it put me in touch with an impressive sense of breadth and strength for the time it was with me. Well over a year later I came across a cryptic passage from Seth that spoke to this issue:

> What you call emotion or feeling ... is the connective
> that most clearly represents the life force on any
> plane, under any circumstances. From it is woven all
> material of your world and mine.[23]

I was almost able to grasp how an elevated state of consciousness could heal or be conveyed to another person, as people find in the presence of saints or great teachers, but I wasn't able to stretch quite that far. I sensed that "feeling" is the common ground, but in this context it included not only what is commonly thought of as emotion but also the complete empathy and identification that equal *knowing*. The otherwise corny line from a popular song came to mind, "If you touch me, you'll understand what happiness is." When the expanded state is firmly established, it is that communicable.

While at the highest levels I remained alert and aware of my surroundings, talking occasionally. Mary was sitting on the floor beside the couch holding my hand, entrained in the stillness. There were times when the music was so enchanting for long passages that if she had moved an inch it would have broken the spell, but she did not, and the experience was deeply affecting.

As the psilocybin performed its mysterious work, I began to sense the subtle, porous interaction of the seen and unseen realities. Useless defenses fell away and I came to feel wide open, vulnerable, and totally "offered up." Those were the peak times, the ones I cherished the most. I hesitated to use the analogy, but I told Mary and Matt, with apologies for the reference, that I felt as if I could lay out my arms and welcome the nails into my hands. This was neither resignation nor sacrifice, but rather a total and joyous surrender to higher powers. No physical threat could have harmed me. Oh, the body may have sensed pain, but the essence of me was immutably safe.

If I found this access with a low dose of an entheogen, I said, the master Jesus surely could have reached a similar attunement at the time of the crucifixion. We mistakenly limit him to our own level if we project that he felt anguish in that situation. I remembered the line from an Ezra Pound poem,

"He cried no cry when they drave the nails." [24]

In that state there is such a deep communion, a resonance, between oneself and the All that the only desire is to join with it. The veil of separation becomes more and more transparent and dissolves almost completely. Cellular consciousness itself expands, the heart opens like a flower in bloom. The individual sense of self blends with the whole so seamlessly that there is no ego, no pride or shame, no need to ask for forgiveness. The pull is so strong that nothing else seems to matter, and in this magnetism one gladly abandons the pettiness of memory and identity. This powerful attraction is the quality I had hoped and even expected to find as the next step toward the God experience when during the first dose of psilocybin I had instead I felt my ego forcefully wrested away. And here at last was the natural transition ... a gentle, beautiful, irresistible call ... a sweet, single note ... your true name ... a gift.

Several times during the day I had the impression of being lovely, graceful, slender and young, dressed in rich robes of satin and jewels. As this great beauty, a vision of the Feminine Ideal, I imagined an encounter with the corresponding Masculine personification in a Celtic setting inspired by the music, dancing outside by firelight. With this came a surprising and charming insight that really I am both in one, and choose to align only with the feminine at this time as a game, an illusion, for the delightful prospect of joining again with the masculine in wholeness.

As in previous sessions, I felt as if physical healing was taking place on a cellular level, although this did not explain why a tendon injury was hurting through the entire process.

I knew that the special qualities and energies of these music selections were now a part of me and would make it easier to recreate the expansion at any time. I will always associate them with my psilocybin experiences.

It was my strong identification with this music throughout the day that evoked the emotion I was contributing to sustain the universe. When the *Selig sind* was played early in the morning, it was so personal that I said I felt as if the angels were singing to welcome me to their world. During another of the choral works it seemed that I was not listening to a recording, but that the piece was being sung to me fresh and current at that very instant, as if it had just burst forth from the higher realms. Even though I'd had altered perceptions of the soundtrack before, this was a new variation.

Part of the enjoyment was "living in the moment," which I probably was able to do only because of my attunement to that kind of music. I felt so relaxed and happy that I told Mary and Matt that I must resolve to have more fun in my life. Like most responsible adults, I had learned it was practical to suppress spontaneity. Instead I should make it a point to appreciate the world of the senses more keenly and to splash in more mud puddles, I said. I remembered the concept of the "holy fool," someone who just acts as he pleases and lets the rest of the world think what they want.

During the session I also commented, "Space-time is vastly overrated." I was quite content in that altered reality.

When I was drifting back toward normal consciousness I discovered one more surprise, a distinct sensation of moving life in my abdomen. It seemed to be a further development of the "program" I felt I had received during my mystical experience, that had appeared as an enameled egg during the following session. I was embarrassed to tell Matt and Mary, but because it was a distinct and notable sensation, I reluctantly spoke up for their records. I also hesitated because it sounded so implausible. Maybe this was being activated ahead of what I would have thought to be its schedule, which I had guessed would be years.

A couple of days later it occurred to me that this movement had been rooted in the same general area as the *hara* which had responded so strongly during the first session. I hoped it was a manifestation of the Living Presence that would in time be thoroughly incorporated, "made flesh."

The session ended quietly. As I filled out the questionnaires, I paused at one of the items and said to Mary, "I never know how to respond to some of these. When I'm asked, 'Do you feel you are superior to other people?' I always hasten to answer No! No! No! On a basic level, I am not. But in another way, I know it's special just to be here."

Roland joined us to review the day. I took a guess that I'd had the low dose, after dealing with two more potent ones and that upsetting initial session. This was now familiar territory, I said, and I had managed it with ease. It just felt like "me, only a little more so" — that is, a deeper expression of me when I'm relaxed and reflective. It was both comfortable and a stretch at the same time.

But the day was growing late. Alida was brought in to join us, and the usual pleasantries were exchanged before we said goodbye. I had just taken my last capsule of psilocybin for the Johns Hopkins research project.

The Missing Coordinate

I was happy and singing as I drove back to Baltimore for my follow-up meeting the next day, as I had usually come to feel on my way to meet with the staff. I titled my required report

"150% of Me" because the experience had seemed to extend and enhance my personality. If my guesses about the dosages I'd received were correct, Matt said, and only the placebo remained, whatever happened during that session would be 100% me, authentic and replicable.

The low dose was like a space station, I told them, providing the appropriate incremental step between my normal waking consciousness and the expanded, celestial me in the more advanced state. This suggested that varying amounts of the entheogen open different levels or intensities of the same alternate reality. As we talked about these effects, Matt noted that I appeared to have mapped the territory of the areas I had explored.

It was reassuring to me that my experiences with the graduated strengths of psilocybin had been consistent and in a direct line on the same trajectory. The low dose was particularly important in helping me assess the accuracy of my starting point (in conventional waking consciousness) in relation to the Divine Presence at the other end of the scale. It also suggested the next step in reconstructing the upward path. I had previously considered that possibility and hoped it would fill in the missing coordinate.

These experiences appeared to confirm that whatever level of understanding I had reached through my years of inquiry was well-grounded, viable, and in close agreement with the reality I had perceived during the action of psilocybin. But I also recognized a problem of self-referencing if it were true that the substance can do no more than amplify and project my own beliefs.

Mary, Matt and I discussed whether the elevated state of consciousness I described was the true and accurate "reality,"

but to the regret of philosophers everywhere we did not resolve that issue. Not counting my first session, by this time
I'd had three experiences at other levels that seemed more in-
cisive and comprehensive than the one from which I began the
journey on the white couch. In each I was able to apprehend
reality more directly than in my normal existence in what
Seth calls a "camouflage universe" where intensities of energy
manifest as events or objects.[25] So once I had returned to this
world of perception limited by the senses, I was eager to learn
to reestablish that other access to knowledge.

After I read aloud my report of the previous day's session,
Mary invited me to add a few more words of explanation about
perceiving the feminine/masculine to be combined as one. She
smiled and said she liked the concept. I didn't recall ever having heard anything like that, I told her. The interpretation had
just surfaced spontaneously, as if it were "given to me." Mary
said, "Yes, by yourself," referring to our discussion on the
source of the messages I had received the day after my mystical
experience.

Mary added that it would be interesting to see what would
happen in the last session. Since I was concentrating on the
four doses of psilocybin, I had nearly forgotten that one more
was scheduled, and was sure that only the placebo remained.
Mary said, "We peeked. You still have the high dose to go." I
was startled for a moment before I realized she was teasing.
She couldn't know that because the study was double-blind.
She did say, though, that volunteers sometimes sensed they
were in altered states after taking the placebo.

When I met with Roland, he advised that my task now
would be to integrate the new insights into my daily life. He
also told me that other volunteers had said that they were so

expanded during their experiences with psilocybin that they never wanted to give up the feeling. Ah, so I wasn't the only one....

A few days later I was unusually open and happy. I felt invigorated, capable, optimistic, and full of energy. Once you have progressed to a certain level by whatever means, I thought, both your Self and the Universe have a considerable investment in keeping you there. It is the "pearl of great price," worth everything. From that perspective, I could better interpret the biblical parable as instruction to simplify one's life as necessary to keep the emphasis on the pearl. But a week later the last remnants of the experience were fading, leaving me foundering, lonely, and yearning for that connection once more.

I wrote a reflection on religious art in my journals. In traditional icons, the saints are portrayed on a gold background meant to convey a supernatural setting. People worship them as having or being something they themselves are unable to achieve. But having had the opportunity to step beyond the commonplace and even temporarily understanding the "saintly" perspective, I could ask those worshippers, "Do you have any idea how close you really are to being that yourself? The potential is already in you, just as the wise ones say. At your core, 'That thou art.' "

Don't Send Me Away!

Another meeting in Baltimore was scheduled at the end of January for the required third-week questionnaires. I arrived on time for my meeting with the staff at 11:00 a.m. and stayed till the end of the day.

After we convened in the session room, with me sitting on

the white couch and Mary and Matt in their accustomed chairs, I related how Lance and I had recently attended a "meet-up" advertised online. We drove to Washington to discuss spirituality and mysticism with others interested in the topics and instead found a large, noisy crowd of young professionals who were concerned mostly with technology and self-promotion. Only a few mentioned spirituality when introducing themselves to the group, and even then we could find no place to talk without screaming. Lance and I gave up and went home, frustrated with the difficulty in connecting with people of like mind.

Matt and Mary invited me to read aloud the additional six-page paper I'd submitted about the recent low-dose session. Matt had some cogent observations about my statement that I was "holding up the world." He seemed to recognize the level I was trying to describe, and his approach from a different perspective gave it a fresh spin.

I told them again how grateful I was to be part of the program. For a week after taking psilocybin, I said, I was still in close touch with the experience, where listening to the same music could recreate much of the atmosphere. After that it became just a pretty tune I associated with a memory. Two weeks later, I was feeling happy, vigorous and productive. By the third week there was no denying that the immediacy of my experience had slipped away, and I began to feel sadness and longing for it. I had found it was not something I could summon again intellectually, like a mathematical formula. Rather, it was a feeling, an accord of the heart, with an evanescent and elusive quality. We instinctively know its power and identify with it, I said, something so natural and fulfilling that we cannot comprehend having lived without it, nor do we ever want to relinquish it. Yet we quickly learn we cannot capture or recreate it by an act of sheer will.

If this had happened at a church or an abbey or a temple, I told them, I would go to the rector and beg to be allowed to remain there. "I will wash dishes and scrub floors, just don't send me away!" But Johns Hopkins is instead a modern, scientific and business institution with a very different mode of operating. I had no recourse. They wouldn't let me stay, even if I chained myself to the couch.

The meeting went on even after Mary's one-hour timer sounded, and I was happy to share more conversation. Afterward, I went back to Mary's office for two hours of filling out questionnaires. While I was still working my way through the stack, Mary noticed the time and said that Roland had only about ten minutes to talk with me before another meeting he had scheduled. I was in his office briefly, and he seemed preoccupied.

Referring to his papers with only an occasional glance at me, Roland asked what I found significant in my fourth session, for which he had recently read my report. I named the highlights, but we did not discuss them. When he inquired about my meditation, I explained that I was continuing on my own. I had not been able to connect with another group, I said, but was still interested in finding one. And with that, my allotted time had expired. As Roland opened his door to show me out, two associates with notebooks were already waiting in the hall to see him.

I finished up my questionnaires in Mary's office and talked with her a little more before a meeting she had scheduled for 4:00 herself. She said that two more volunteers had begun actively working with this second study, and the last two of eighteen were being selected. The research team had already seen some of the early volunteers for their one-year follow-up interviews.

Feeling a little wistful, I told Mary that although I could have predicted my life before I joined the program, I truly did not see how anything could remain the same after this, nor would I want it to. Mary understood my concern about separating from the project after such intense personal involvement, but life would go on, she said, even though I might not be able to foresee the details.

Philosophizing With Matt

As I finished up with Mary, I asked if Matt might have a few minutes to meet with me so we could try to reconstruct his earlier insight about the level where emotion supports the world. Matt was gracious about making time to talk. He apologized for the clutter in his office, consisting of nothing more than some skewed stacks of paper, as we settled in to the two desk chairs for a conversation.

When I invited him to elaborate on his earlier comments, he said it seemed I had been sensitive to a state of consciousness from which the universe was constantly manifesting, where I participated directly in its creative and sustaining forces. Before that particular experience, this wasn't anything familiar to me through my reading, although it fit in with my general cosmology. I appreciated that Matt was willing to acknowledge both the existence of such a state and that I could have touched into it. I was also impressed that with his background in chemistry and psychology he seemed equally at ease with the concepts of metaphysics.

I reminded him that although I had been forewarned

about demons and psychological traps, I'd had only positive experiences during the psilocybin sessions, after trouble with the initial dose, and was pleased to find myself an integrated personality under those conditions. He said, "Yeah, you've gone from cellar to ceiling in there with a flashlight and haven't turned up anything bad." The image made me laugh.

Matt marveled aloud that such a small amount of physical matter could cause such sweeping changes in consciousness. How does an entheogen affect the body, he asked rhetorically, and how does the body determine states of consciousness? He pulled a book off the shelf and showed me diagrams of the psilocybin molecule, amazed that something so simple could have such a profound influence.

Matt also talked about the varieties of experience with that entheogen and told me they are not universally interpreted as religious. Some people just want to get high at a concert, he said. "Kids take this at raves." But without a spiritual context, he added, the response was more likely to be, "Duuude, the room is melting!" I was surprised to hear that anyone could walk around and function with it in their system, since I was hardly able to get off the couch. And they can actually buy this on the street?

I believed that the revelations of psilocybin were of benefit both to me and through me, somehow, to the world in general. Yet it was difficult to justify a sense of achievement when I was so physically compromised and unproductive while the substance was active. Since we have agreed to the terms of three-dimensional existence, dealing with our world this way seems the responsible thing to do. Practical action has every contrast with feeling attuned to other levels in an altered state caused by hallucinogens, or in a passive contemplation of the

Divine. That also begs the question of how it can be useful to sit in meditation.

Matt offered a perspective that helped me better evaluate the issue. He cited theories that a person in touch with those higher energies is actually grounding them in the "biological vessel," an excellent description of the body's role. Such a commingling may not create matter or directly result in corporal activity, but its influence can inspire us to bring powerful forces into manifestation. This elevated level of being, which I had fleetingly glimpsed, is the source, the blueprint, of all that comprises us and continually appears as the reality we consider so solid. I recalled that ancient and modern philosophers have declared plainly that "thoughts are things."

Matt quoted back to me the phrase from my dream about being "completely supported even when there is no visible evidence." Though our ability to perform physical functions in these states may be limited temporarily, the insights remain with us to inform all subsequent action, so that the effects of a moving entheogenic experience become expressed later as changes in behavior. The resulting benefit of tapping into such dimensions was often cited by the staff: "Altered traits, not altered states." [26]

Wrapping up our conversation, Matt also suggested the attitude that makes this possible, "a self-exploration with seriousness and reverence." I felt grateful to have this conversation with him and was glad to count him as both a philosophical and professional ally.

There was something else bothering me, though. I admitted that I didn't understand how the researchers could talk so freely about spiritual matters which by nature seemed subjective. "You're scientists," I said. "You measure things. How can an institution like Johns Hopkins deal with such unquantifiable subjects?"

"It's okay," Matt assured me with a smile. "We're psychologists. Roland is a Professor of Behavioral Biology, and I consider myself primarily a psychologist, studying mind and behavior. We're allowed to talk about such things as emotions and relationships and spirituality."

Matt escorted me down to the lobby and I signed out at the end of the workday. I walked across the parking lot with my coat blowing open in the harsh, cold wind just to celebrate the sensations of being on the earth. As I turned my car down the hill to leave, gray clouds hinted at snow. Before I had driven a half-mile, a flurry of delicate flakes was swirling around the car — a beautiful ending to a beautiful day.

I still had a 95-mile drive ahead of me through heavy traffic in the dark. After I left the city, I pulled into a parking lot for a quick nap before I could resume the trip and take care of my errands, and arrived home just after 10:00 p.m. I had many physical surges throughout the evening, and welcomed them as signs of fresh energy from my exchanges that day.

CHAPTER 9

One Just to Love

Within a week it was time to return to Baltimore for my final scheduled psilocybin session, a Tuesday early in February. I'd already had four uncommon day-long experiences, which meant only the placebo could be available. It seemed a nuisance to have someone take me to the appointment when I was sure I'd be capable of driving home afterward, but by then I knew it was futile to try to bend the rules of the research project.

I got up at 2:30 a.m. to get ready for the day, and left the house in bitter wind for an hour's drive to my sister Lisa's home. She was kind enough to take me on to Baltimore, and we arrived in time for my 8:00 appointment.

All the preparations were routine, and just as strict as if I were liable to get an active dose. I signed in at the front desk, was escorted upstairs, and submitted a urine sample.

When I met with Roland, he counseled that my behavior was still under scrutiny and I should not assume that I knew how the day's events would proceed. This was consistent with Mary's caution that sometimes volunteers had vivid experiences in a placebo session. I welcomed the advice, but didn't see how

I could possibly encounter anything except plain old ordinary reality that day. In any case, I am usually at ease in quiet situations, so I did not expect to be bored or fidgety during the placebo session, though deprived of visual references and the activity of psilocybin. I even wondered if I could sneak in a nap after starting the day so early.

As Mary accompanied me to the inner room, that familiar wave of apprehension began to build, the respect for the process beyond my control. I was well aware that it was a privilege to be there once again with those three trusted guides around me. Tears came to my eyes. No matter what happened, I knew, it would be my last day on the white couch, so my sense of loss was as strong as my sense of anticipation.

After I took the capsule in the little ceremony, I asked to read a poem I had been reworking for days, titled "Love Song to J.H." I spoke the words solemnly, repeating the verse about the strangely satisfying evolution from "knowing" to "not knowing," and gave the copy to the staff to add to my file.

When Roland had returned to his office, I sat with Mary and Matt on the couch to look through a book. Even though I felt no changes, after a while we agreed to begin the procedures, and I put on the eye mask and headphones. I was hoping that merely being in the setting would allow me to find my way back to the same elevated states as previous occasions there, but that did not happen. Instead the session evolved easily and simply, free of expectation, and in the company of friends.

This was the day to sink into the music without any concern that I was being manipulated into a response. Every time I heard a selection that I thought would be the pinnacle, I would become just as immersed in the next piece, and then the next. Again I admired those composers who are able to capture those states and express them in a medium others can share. To me it seems the highest and most mysterious of the arts. Because I had such a resonance with the kind of music on the soundtrack, I could easily allow it to direct my attention. And, happily, I had nothing to do all day but enjoy it.

During the *Selig sind,* I said that I never feel so close to the upper realms as when I hear that work. The singers, those invisible angels, seemed to dwell there, while I was only visiting. I long to remain there, but in supernatural light, not the darkness of the eye mask.

While the repetitious thrums of one of the Gorecki songs played on, I could sense a series of healing pulses emanating from me out into the world. My personal strength and projected power seemed to increase with the rhythms of another work, and it was thrilling to hear the rich, vibrant tones that gave the Bach *Passacaglia* its color. When composers build up to a crescendo or a level of intensity, I like to observe how they gracefully restore the motion afterward.

Occasionally I would find myself refocusing on my physical presence in the room after being lost in imagination. I had no indications of having taken a hallucinogen; it was just the indulgence of a mind that was free from fear, worry, or an immediate task.

After my first lunch during a session, both Mary and Matt sat beside the couch and held my hands as the spell of the music joined us in the same space. Yes, I'd made rewarding journeys with psilocybin, but being deeply moved by emotions and friendship was every bit as authentic, and reliably more replicable. These, too, were moments to be treasured.

At one point in the day I was reflecting on my relationship

with my mother. I remembered that when she was 45 years old
and had seven children, the youngest of whom was finally in
school, she was upset to discover that she was pregnant again.
Although she had been depressed at the prospect of having to
raise yet another child, she later said, "God gave me one just to
love" when the others were old enough to take care of themselves. I told Matt and Mary that my day with the placebo was
much the same. After all the demands of dealing with psilocybin, I had a day "just to love," appreciating the music and
the companionship.

Late in the afternoon, after I had put on my lenses and
brushed my hair, I completed the day's questionnaires. When
Roland rejoined us and asked about the session, I told him
how relaxed it had been and how much I'd enjoyed the company and the soundtrack. He said, "Well, then I guess you've
passed."

"So I've successfully completed the program?"

"Yes," he smiled, "You've graduated."

Again I expressed my sadness and loss at separating from
this project which had given me so much affirmation and expansion. Roland insisted that my experience did not originate
with the entheogen or depend on their program, that these
merely reveal to me my own being and my potential. He gazed
across the room at nothing in particular and expressed his philosophy quietly and firmly. "It's not Johns Hopkins, it's not the
staff, it's not the pill — it's in *you*." He wanted to be clear that
what I sought, I already had. I understood that intellectually,
but my emotions were having a field day of denial, and I knew
I would be working through the issue for some time to come.
As Roland described it, we all came together "in a dance" for
the study, each playing his own part. This one was ending, but

I had to believe that there would be another dance for me sometime, somewhere.

Lisa was escorted upstairs to meet with the staff before we left. During our drive home in the dark, we stopped for dinner and I treated. When I got a craving for ice cream after we were on the road again, we pulled in to a convenience store to raid the freezer. This time, Lisa treated. "Here, let me buy you a graduation present," she said.

I slept well at Lisa's that night and wrote up my notes on her computer. There was a fresh dusting of snow the next morning as I drove to Baltimore for my day-after appointment.

I had a good meeting with Mary and Matt, as usual, and read them my report about the previous day. When I got to the part about it being my last session, I found myself in tears and had to pause before I could resume.

Mary told me that during my first psilocybin session I'd had one of the strongest reactions to the substance that she and Matt had seen. This included not just the physical impact that day, but the extended emotional effects and the slow return to normal life. Matt attributed the prolonged recovery to my larger psychological response to the experience, the way one would get over a fright or an accident. Mary said they had known I was vacillating about continuing, and after meeting with me they had guessed at the odds that I would remain in the program. Both agreed that I was courageous to come back and try again, so they were all the more pleased when I responded so positively in the second session. I was grateful for their compliments and their empathy with my situation. Mary said that some of the other volunteers also had faced difficulties, but still valued their experiences.

I was looking forward to my meeting with Roland that

day, too, but he was busy with phone calls and could not make time for me.

Mary set up two further appointments, one in two weeks and another two weeks beyond that. These would be brief, but would help ease my departure from the program. And then I found myself stepping out the door, starting my car, heading home. There would be no psilocybin expansion to relish for days, no friendly faces for support and sharing.

Closer to Parting

It was difficult to turn my attention away from the project, especially after the revelations it had brought. I reminded myself that communion with the Divine did not come from a capsule, that it was the underlying definition of my Self, and the entheogen simply enabled temporary conscious access. "It's in you." Jesus says that. Bartholomew says that. Joel Goldsmith says that. Roland says that. Everyone says that — and it had already had been unequivocally demonstrated to me.

I understood this as an aspect of the spiritual principle that all is one substance. We can learn to open to all being and potential, but only to the extent we are aware that we are part of it. In a cartoon I'd once drawn to remind myself of this, I had pictured myself in ragged clothes in a crumbling apartment, wringing a handkerchief and sobbing. The caption was, "Maria has forgotten about her Mediterranean villa." Now I had come back to the same point: knowing the touchstone of power was within me, but still unsure how to find the connection. I knew that if I were just able to activate it, then all my desires would be fulfilled. But that self-realization seemed far away, achievable only by the masters.

By the time I met with Matt and Mary for a follow-up

visit two weeks later, I was dealing better with the situation. I told them about my recent visit to a Christian meditation center in Washington as I continued to search for a group where I was comfortable. Toward the end of our one-hour meeting in the session room, Mary invited me to choose a piece of music from the soundtrack, so we could sit together quietly. I picked Sir Edward Elgar's *Nimrod*.

After that, Roland met with me privately in Mary's office, which I took to mean his chairs were overflowing with papers. He began with the general "How are you feeling?" and "Any more insights?" We discussed my sadness over leaving the program, and I said I'd done some introspection about why I was finding it so difficult emotionally. I usually have more composure than that.

When I was six years old, I told him, my mother walked me down to the road and put me on the school bus, and nothing's been the same since then. There were twelve years of school, four years of college, and forty-odd years of business work. As soon as I retired I became immersed in the States of Consciousness Research Project. So now I was not only finishing the program I had loved so much, I was coming to the close of all the social structure I could remember since I started first grade. Roland acknowledged that this was a major transition in my life.

The facts I'd outlined were true, but I was shifting the emphasis to an organizing principle I thought he would value. I didn't expect to miss the structure all that much, and was actually very happy to be eliminating so much of it. I just wanted to salvage a little pride and appear adaptable and self-sufficient.

Once I had finished my meetings at Bayview, I barely had

time to get directions from Matt and rush across town to keep an appointment with Dr. Richards, whom I had not seen since my initial interview in the summer. Because everyone on the staff called him "Bill," it was difficult to decide how to address him, but I reverted to "Dr. Richards."

I was happy to visit with him again after seven months. He asked about my general experiences in the program, since he had not read my reports. I described my distress and recovery from the first session and my joy at the transcendence in the second, saying how much I wished I could hold onto it for the rest of my life. I was somewhat surprised when he suggested that I should let go, trust that it will stay with me, and watch for the next thing to come along.

I also thanked him for the beautiful music he had organized into the soundtrack for the sessions. He told me the *Selig sind* was regarded as a favorite for accompanying hallucinogenic experiences, making it a gift to generations of seekers. I couldn't resist asking why the opening movement of Brahms' powerful Symphony No. 1 was also played early in the day. Since I'd first encountered it in their program, I had heard other recordings of the same piece that didn't have nearly the drama, so it must have been chosen for its impact.

Dr. Richards pointed out that the volunteer is undergoing his most serious psychological challenges at that time, so the music is intended to provide firm, supportive, nonverbal structure. Some volunteers accept its steady, forward-moving rhythms as an embrace to propel them beyond their fears and resistances, he said. As for explaining my reaction, he allowed, "It doesn't work for everyone." He also pointed out that a person does not always respond to a particular piece of music the same way each time.

As we said goodbye, he recommended that I play those Chopin nocturnes I liked on the piano as a form of meditation. I was pleased he had remembered this from our first visit and I was glad to hear such a broad definition of meditation. When I got back to the car, I just sat for a few minutes and tried to let the reality of these final moments sink in.

I called to check in with Alida on the way home. She reminded me that this was Shrove Tuesday, the day before Lent began, which meant Lance would be fixing his excellent homemade pancakes. I stopped by for a good dinner and visit with him that evening. It was a rare occasion when none of his family was home and the house was quiet, so we enjoyed a leisurely talk.

For the next two weeks I was left to ruminate about having only one more meeting scheduled in Baltimore and about my lack of progress at meditation. I would try to sit quietly to develop this new practice, but there seemed to be no way to guarantee good results, to devise a formula, or to speed up the learning process. I couldn't force the issue or summon a higher state at will, and obviously there was no way to *think* myself into it. Sometimes I would feel an attunement, and at others it seemed that heaven had turned me out the same as the research program had.

I was trying to determine whether this would require continuing hard work or perhaps only realigning my attitude. Don't people dedicate their lives to reaching that state because it's so inaccessible? Yet great teachers say that it's available to each of us every instant. I had actually been there, and now couldn't figure out how to return to it, or how to ease the frustration that resulted. I suspected that trying too hard would be counterproductive, but the right balance was elusive.

Is This an Addiction?

Even though thoughts about these subjects dominated my days, I shared them with only a few people. One was a friend from my travels in Arizona who was pleased to hear that I'd had a mystical experience. But she was also concerned because it had come from "drugs," and moreover that I was willing to do it again. She worked in a municipal courts system where she routinely confronted the social consequences of substance abuse, so she worried that I would become addicted.

"Yes, I want to be in that state again," I told her, "but I really don't feel a physical craving for psilocybin — it can be very demanding — and I don't believe that's the only way to have such an experience." The researchers had been clear that psilocybin was safe and non-addictive, I told her, but I realized that my explanation didn't sound very convincing. The person taking heroin probably just wants to recreate the state he was in, too.

This made me wonder whether the definition was in the physical or the mental response. Can someone become dependent after only four doses, more than a month apart? Did I have to start snatching purses and embezzling money for drugs before I'd be considered an addict? The conundrum brought to mind the Catholic doctrine that just *wanting* to commit the act was a sin. I emailed these questions to the Johns Hopkins staff, and Matt promptly sent back a very practical reply to relieve any anxiety.

> There are accepted criteria that psychologists and psychiatrists follow in determining if a person qualifies for a diagnosis of substance dependence (this is the current accepted scientific name for 'addiction').

Briefly, it requires that the drug use has led to *clinically significant* impairment or distress, as manifested by at least three of the following symptoms within the same 12-month period (criteria are abbreviated to their basic elements):

1. Tolerance
2. Withdrawal
3. Often taking more of the drug or taking it for a longer time than intended
4. Persistent desire to cut down your drug use or unsuccessful attempts to cut down drug use
5. A great deal of time devoted to obtaining the drug
6. Giving up or reducing important social, occupational, or recreational activities
7. Continued use despite knowledge of a physical or psychological problem the drug use has caused

Reading over these, I think you will agree you are unambiguously not drug dependent. Even before we get to the specific criteria, you would not qualify for drug dependence because your use has not appeared to have caused a clinically significant impairment of your life functioning. This is the same as what your gut was telling you when you noted that you are not stealing purses or embezzling money to get drugs....

As an aside, you are correct that drug dependence does not necessarily require 'physical dependence.' Only the withdrawal and tolerance criteria are considered forms of physical dependence, so they may or may not be present in drug dependence. For example, most heroin addicts are physically dependent, while most cocaine addicts are not physically dependent, even though both drugs can certainly lead to drug dependence. Regardless, you would not qualify for either form of drug dependence.... In this case, the terminology only provides words (and possibly not the best ones) for what your own intuition tells you.

Once again, the staff had quickly responded to my needs. I sensed that Matt had simplified his answer to me and that he was brimming with other data and explanations, but this addressed the issue adequately.

Commencement

My last meeting in Baltimore was in early March 2007, on a sunny, cold, and windy day. I arrived for my 10:30 appointment with a few minutes to spare before the security personnel rang for Mary. We joined Matt in the session room and settled in for a short meditation before our talk. I had taken the initiative of writing a final report, and at Mary's request I read it aloud, which took about twenty minutes with my personal remarks. Matt was always interested in the titles I chose. This one was "Commencement."

When I came to the description of the transcendental experience in the second session ("in that state there are no questions, there are no desires, there is no resistance") my voice broke with emotion, even though nearly five months had passed since that remarkable event. It wasn't only that I was sitting on the same couch in the same room with the same two people as when it happened. I had reviewed the draft of my report the day before and choked up at exactly that place. If just the memory of that hour could have such an effect on me, could anyone doubt the power of the experience itself?

Mary said that as I was reading she began to notice I hadn't quoted Bartholomew, I hadn't quoted Joel. "This is quite an exception to some of your reports."

"I've always said that I quote when I have no firsthand knowledge," I told her. "But this was *my* report. Bart and Joel didn't have those experiences — I did." Psychologists observe that every toddler is doing original research into the nature of the universe. By the same standard, I was the first explorer ever to reach an altered state. No guide could have prepared me for it or accompanied me. I had emerged feeling stronger and more capable, and drawn forward to further discoveries.

I admitted frankly that I would welcome an occasional refresher dose of psilocybin. I'd recognized mental and physical similarities every time I'd taken the substance, and my body had come to tolerate it. But I assured Mary and Matt I would not take street drugs, for reasons much more compelling than respect for legal status. The issues of substance purity and personal monitoring are certainly a concern. But more important, I need to *know* — truly, beyond the shadow of a doubt — that I can connect with that state on my own, that I can find the route within my psyche. My ideal experience must be wholly owned, "authentic and replicable" in Matt's words.

The goal then becomes nothing short of mysticism, the direct perception of the Divine. Many teachings say that this communion can be reached by a natural, integrated spiritual development, with the gift of grace. In oversized type in the final report, centered prominently on the page, I wrote, "I need to know that I am a child of God and not a child of hallucinogens. If I will not accept a church as an intermediary to God, why would I accept a hallucinogen?"

I told Mary and Matt that my efforts to open to that level again would include my favorite practice, spiritual reading. I have always found excellent guidance in print. Books have reliably provided inspiration as well as information when I knew no other source, and appropriate books have come to me at every stage. Meditation would be a staple, too; I had adopted this almost as soon as it was recommended when the sessions began. I also felt more of a desire for friendship on the path, I told them, and I wanted to seek out compatible persons or groups.

In the report I stated that I can rely on several traits in my search for spiritual progress: my intuition is sound, I am willing to learn and to work, and I am sincere. These qualities, plus continuously accumulating knowledge and experience, will serve me well.

After I had spent two hours completing the third-week questionnaires, Mary walked me down the hall to Roland's office. I was talking with her about how everything seemed to come to a halt for me now that the program was ending. It felt like that moment when the pendulum reaches its farthest point and pauses a moment in suspension before resuming motion. I mused aloud that I thought the word was "equipoise."

Just then Roland came up the hallway and escorted me into his office. I took a seat by his desk, separated from him as usual by several tall stacks of paper, and mentioned that although I had learned a great deal, I was feeling undirected, uncertain about what to do next. I asked, "Is there such a word as equipoise?"

"Yes," he said, moving his hands to demonstrate the equilibrium between actions. "Spiritual seekers value it greatly and strive to reach it."

"Well, that's where I am." I said. "It seems kind of like the void."

"And the void is the source of all new principle and creativity," Roland offered.

I knew I should be grateful for the respite, but I just felt lost. When Roland inquired about work or leisure activities that I might be looking forward to, I told him I was more free than I had been in fifty-some years, and although I had many appealing choices, nothing in particular had emerged as the obvious next step.

A Portal of Light

However, I did have a question for him that afternoon. I opened Eckhart Tolle's book *The Power of Now*, which I knew he had read, and turned to a passage about a portal of radiant light at the time of death. Tolle says that joining with this light, which the Tibetans call "the luminous splendor of the colorless light of Emptiness," brings conscious immortality, yet because of fear and resistance most people turn away from it unless they had encountered this dimension in their lifetime. When this brief opportunity passes unheeded, they fall back into relative unconsciousness and continue with further incarnations.[27]

I asked Roland, "Do you think that is the Light I saw in my transcendental state?" He agreed that, yes, he thought it was. I closed the book and reminded him I'd said at the time that many aspects were like the classic description of a near-death experience.

Then I pressed the issue a little more. "So do you think I may have an advantage, and after death I will recognize the Light again and be able to join with it directly?"

I expected him to say that seemed likely, but instead he

described the Tibetan practice of preparing for thirty or forty years to maximize that very moment of death with the intention of joining the Light. Some devotees achieve such a discipline that they can make their departure a conscious act, Roland told me. He put his hands together in the traditional prayer gesture and touched them to his forehead, saying, "I'm out of here."

"Mahasamadhi," I said. He looked at me with what I took to be a little surprise that I would know the word for that and repeated knowingly, "Mahasamadhi."

Roland's characteristic caution seemed to imply that I probably wouldn't be prepared that well and would miss the opportunity. I told him that nevertheless I would be looking for that Light all my life and especially at the moment of death. At least I got *some* kind of concession from him. I didn't think it would be as difficult to bargain with St. Peter himself.

However, I was not convinced that this Light is available to only the spiritually prepared elite. If truck drivers and housewives, not just monks and masters, come back from near-death experiences raving about the Light that they did not want to leave, it doesn't seem so exceptional to consciously discover it at that time. None of these ordinary people has studied arcane teachings for decades, yet they appear to be just as welcome in the sight of the Divine. "Go to the Light!" has become nearly a cliché about death. Neither Roland nor the Tibetans seemed to be claiming so much that God is inaccessible as that we are uninformed or unaware. But perhaps God is more generous and we are more perceptive than either of them surmise.

As our meeting concluded, I repeated my thanks for being accepted into the States of Consciousness project, and said I hoped my participation had contributed to their study. Roland spoke enthusiastically about the work. "This is the first time this type of research is being done on these drugs in thirty years. At last we are so close to answering basic questions about how hallucinogens affect the human psyche and explaining the mysteries of the mind." He seemed pleased with progress in the research and optimistic about the contributions the Johns Hopkins studies would make to knowledge in the field. I was happy enough to be a footnote. Our conversation went on only a little longer, then Roland stood up, my cue that the meeting was over.

Mary walked me down to the lobby and we talked for a few more minutes. I admitted that I felt a little lost without immediate plans but was willing to allow the next events to unfold in their own good time. It was a bittersweet moment, despite all Mary's good wishes. With a final embrace, we parted and I stepped out into the chilly air. The sun was edging closer to the horizon. I sat in the car for a few minutes, incredulous that my part in the project had been completed, and tried to get myself together before I headed home. By my count I had made 25 trips to Baltimore over the course of my application and participation in the study, about 5,000 miles in 10 months.

I needed to remember that I was learning to be open to the Divine, however it manifested, and that this goal must not become secondary to remaining in the favor of the States of Consciousness researchers. It was wrenching to break those ties, but I am supposed to be living in the *now*, not in memories of the past or fantasies of the future, and any moment could bring fresh insight and revelation. That intention could keep me occupied very thoroughly.

CHAPTER 10

After a Year

All five psilocybin sessions and their follow-ups were complete, but there would be one more meeting when I returned to Baltimore for my final review a year later. In the meantime, adjusting to life without the program was difficult. I was a textbook example of frustration, lack of discipline, and self-criticism for not being able to release my connection with Johns Hopkins, which was all the more vexing because I had known the separation was inevitable. Like watching a car headed for a cliff, all I could do was roll the camera and say, "Wow, there it goes."

Mary had confided that I was not the only volunteer who'd had difficulty leaving the program, although she said nothing further about the persons or circumstances. She also told me that the guidelines discouraged the staff from keeping in close touch with volunteers, especially during the first year after they completed the program. She let me know she would be available if I needed to contact her, and assured me we were still on good terms. But the point was clear — it would be up to me to reestablish my balance, and then to put my new knowledge into practice.

I had hopes of learning a method quickly to help with the adjustment. In discussions with the staff I had become aware of the research of Stanislav Grof in developing a "holotropic" breathing technique to reach altered states. I found a class advertised on the Internet and signed up for a full-day workshop scheduled about six weeks after I finished the program in Baltimore.

I made sure to arrive on time for the introductory talk the night before the workshop. Just over a dozen people would be attending. Many of them had been through the breathwork program with these guides before, which seemed a good recommendation. The practical instructions were barely covered that evening, but I thought I would learn them from observation the next day. During free time to get acquainted, I was the subject of some attention when I mentioned I'd recently completed the States of Consciousness project. Three other people there told me they'd applied unsuccessfully and wanted to know what it was like.

Before the workshop began the next morning each of us teamed up with a partner. One would be the subject (reclining on a floor mat) and one the monitor during the morning, and we'd switch roles for the afternoon. I chose to be the monitor first so I could watch the process. The two facilitators rolled out large amplifiers, turned up some Indian music to an ear-splitting volume, and dimmed the lights until the room was almost dark. The active subjects started their special breathing methods and were soon writhing, sobbing, and sometimes screaming. One of the guides smiled with satisfaction and moved with the music as she walked around shouting, "Let it all out! Scream louder!"

I was trying to be open-minded — after all, many of these

people had paid to come back and do this again — but I was horrified at what I saw. Compared to the careful preparation and supervision I'd had at Johns Hopkins, this looked patently irresponsible and dangerous. I barely managed to persevere through the morning's activities, with tissue stuffed in my ears, because I felt an obligation to my partner going through the procedures, but there was no way I could participate in or even watch the afternoon session. I still shudder to remember it as "a discothèque in hell." Maybe not all such workshops were conducted this way, but I did not understand the breathwork theory and, based on that day's demonstration, I was not inclined to inquire further.

My next-best hope for reaching an altered state reliably had just evaporated. Without that option or hallucinogens, the most likely method for attaining higher states was going to be meditation. That looked like serious, long-term work, not exactly instant gratification.

I was still searching for a meditation group, but felt an uncomfortable cultural gap with Eastern practices. After an online query I found a Christian-oriented group 70 miles away in Washington. Starting while I was still in the research project, I attended a number of their Sunday morning gatherings. I enjoyed the meetings with a small number of university students, but after a few months they dispersed when the school year ended and their capable director moved away. From then on, I just set aside time for this at home.

There were not many notable events for me in the year that followed the study, either in my personal circumstances or my spiritual life. I endured a dawn-to-dusk racket as the state highway department reconfigured and widened the road beside my property during the spring, summer, and fall. As the protective trees fell to the bulldozers, I tried to regard it as a lesson in acceptance, when I'd purposely chosen a home out of view.

By fall I was beginning to feel a restlessness and lack of progress, socially or spiritually. In similar situations I have often delayed or avoided action when I didn't feel a driving passion or couldn't see a linear goal; the result was usually further stagnation. This time I thought I would just try movement for the sake of movement. In an effort to get the energy flowing again, it almost didn't matter how, I decided to sign up for an art class.

I committed to a 60-mile drive for a six-session watercolor course to renew my enjoyment of the medium. Feeling more confident after that, I taught a small class in beginning watercolor in a community education program. This was my first experience with teaching any subject, and I liked the aspect of sharing information that could change and enrich lives. The students were responsive and made steady improvements.

In the winter, I worked for two months for my former employer while a few staff members were out, then was persuaded to continue working there two days a week. I was enjoying retirement and was reluctant to take on a regular schedule again, but my need for income trumped the call of leisure.

These small adjustments in my life did not amount to the kind of drama I guess I was hoping for — after all, the States of Consciousness project was a hard act to follow. And yet, I reminded myself, excitement and glamour were not the object. I had not yet told three of my brothers and most of my office associates about my involvement in the study. It was easier than having to deal with bad jokes about drugs or blank stares on the subject of spirituality.

My daily meditation did not seem to bring me much closer to the deep, still, mindless states that are its goal. Joel Goldsmith's instructions to approach meditation without pre-conceptions, like an explorer in an unknown land,[28] sounded like similar advice from the staff before the psilocybin sessions. I also took solace in Joel's statement that the fruits of meditation do not necessarily appear during the meditation itself,[29] because often I could detect no change. If anything, I was feeling the frustration of a child needing to be shown yet again how to tie his shoes. Even the memory of that conscious Divine Presence was beginning to slip away.

I had encouragement from books by two of my favorite teachers on the possibility of reaching that state again through my initiative. Seth had said:

> If there is any point where your own consciousness seems to elude you or escape you, or if there is any point where your consciousness seems to end, then these are the points where you have yourselves set up psychological and psychic barriers, and these are pre-cisely those areas you should explore.[30]

Bartholomew addressed the subject more specifically and supported my own intuition:

> ... drugs blast open a part of your energy field which you could open on your own if you had the deter-mination to do so.... Any opening you have, in what you call an altered state, is also available to you in the natural state.... Do not get dependent on something outside yourself to give you the experiences you are looking for.[31]

The Divine in Form

As I considered my experiences with psilocybin in the light of further readings and reflections, I became better able to identify the spiritual aspect of ego, and after some effort I also improved my grasp on the concept of awareness. At least I was starting to notice when I was being judgmental, which was pretty much all of the time, even if I was nowhere near overcoming it.

And then a dazzling insight gradually dawned on me. For most of my life I had accepted the dour Christian teaching that on earth we are banished from our true home. I'd made amazing discoveries during my psilocybin sessions, and had been only too quick to assume that the different reality I had experienced was more true, more significant, and more accurately heaven-like than the three-dimensional world I took for granted. But then a new viewpoint began to emerge and I was able to look out on that world with a fresh perspective.

Right in my home and yard were wonders just as vital, as rich, as the realms of psilocybin. Beautiful sunlight that you can see but can't capture. Magical water, in all its changing forms. Plants growing from tiny seeds. The pleasure of good food that you start to draw in with the mere aroma. The incredible medium of music that can stir such profound sentiments. The joys of companionship, the sweet affection of a pet, the contrast of day and night, the change of seasons, the sensations of a brisk walk or a warm bath, watching the landscape zip by as you drive. And the most intimate but incomprehensible example, so close we miss it, the functioning and continuous renewal of our own bodies. All of these are just as remarkable as the reality revealed by hallucinogens, the only difference is that we have ceased to notice them. They are no less miraculous for being physical and for being familiar.

Without doubt, it had been spectacular to delve into a different state of consciousness, but it was at least as moving to realize the delight, the honor, and the inconceivable *privilege* of living on the earth. I began to see that our sojourn here is not a mistake, not an exile. Each of us had to apply for it, qualify for it, yearn for it so intensely that we became flesh. Then we bravely and willingly closed the door behind us to guarantee our total immersion in this appearance of separation.

It is incorrect to suppose we can't know why we're here. We can recall our attraction with a little concentration, not just because it was once our choice, but because we are still choosing it in every instant. We were not put here for penance and suffering. Our purpose was not just to have an opportunity to learn in Schoolroom Earth, or even to labor in the vineyards and contribute our personal experiences to enrich the whole. In a moment of clarity I understood that every soul incarnates out of sheer exuberance. Knowing it is forever safe, free, and grounded in love, the oversoul sends an aspect of itself on an adventurous romp in space-time. We are not outcasts or prisoners, but naturally inquisitive and joyous creatures who want the diversion and the thrill. We are, as they say, gods in training who enjoy the challenge of mastering the illusion and are learning to create consciously within it.

Having had an opportunity, with the assistance of psilocybin, to look back through that door from which we came, I could cherish this dimension all the more. Suddenly I began to appreciate the intense focus required to maintain our orientation here. This perspective inspires us to value the magnificent vehicle of the body, shun restriction and false asceticism, enjoy sensual delights, and welcome every opportunity to laugh, to share, to love, and to dance. It does not excuse us from striving to learn and grow or from assuming personal responsibility, but it can restore a balance too easily lost in our ambition for security and esteem.

In the end, there is no separation between the sacred and the secular, between thought and action, between spirituality and science. What better example than the astonishing fact that energy equals mass times the speed of light squared? We will come to see that the illusion is not physical existence but rather the notion of separation itself. It is not a dichotomy of the Divine *and* form. The world around us is simply the Divine *in* form, an aspect of All That Is as it manifests under conditions we call time and space.

This interpretation is firmly rooted in principles that Seth, Spangler, and others describe and that I had long accepted, but had not "seen from the inside." Certainly this surprising realization was easier to comprehend after having experienced more than one version of reality, but it did not occur to me until at least six months after my mystical vision. As I told Mary later, "It's a song I will be singing the rest of my life."

Back to Baltimore at Last

Spring couldn't come soon enough because that meant I'd be visiting the research staff again. I had exchanged emails with Mary occasionally during the intervening year, and even with Matt once or twice.

I was delighted when Mary phoned to make my appointment for early March. She wanted to know in which of the sessions I thought I'd had the two highest doses. Without hesitation I answered, "The first and second." She paused a moment and said, "That's right."

I didn't understand why she would ask — we'd been over that so many times. But I saw the reason when she mailed me the Retrospective Questionnaire the following week. The first item, which Mary had already filled in, read, "You received the two highest dose levels of psilocybin on the two sessions listed below (at this time we cannot reveal which dose was given on which session)." Mary had written "Sessions 1 and 2" in the blanks in accordance with my answers to her phone inquiry. The next item asked, "Do these two sessions correspond to your memory of the two sessions in which you had the most pronounced changes in your ordinary mental processes? Yes/ No. [If 'No,' do not complete this questionnaire until talking with us.]"

Following this were 17 pages inquiring about my memory of the sessions (Feelings of timelessness? Sense of reverence?), persisting effects, my attitudes about self and life, behavior, moods, relationships, and spiritual matters such as prayer, death, and perception of God — the kind of form I had filled out many times for the project. As had happened so often before, I found myself in a quandary when asked if, for instance, spirituality had become a more central (or, the next question would ask, less central) part of my life. I wanted to write in, "It was always pretty darn central, and if it hadn't been before, psilocybin would have seen to that!" But all they wanted was a plain checkmark for yes or no.

I completed over 180 questions that required a quantifying number (0 for "none" to 5 for "extreme"). Now, for the first time, there were blank lines to write out personal responses. One of the items addressed a major issue: "Would you want to take psilocybin again, assuming that you could do so under lawful circumstances?" There were three categories of answers to choose from: (1) No, never. (Subchoices included "too risky, too unpleasant, too intense, too much effort, and not meaningful to repeat the experience.") (2) Possibly, perhaps sometime in the future, and (3) Yes. (Subchoices included "I would consider taking it again with a guide, on my own without a guide, as part of a spiritual/religious group, or traveling to another country in order to take it lawfully.") There wasn't much debate in my mind, but I wondered how other volunteers answered. I finished the questionnaire carefully to take back to Baltimore for my appointment.

So, on a Tuesday in March 2008, one year and six days after last seeing the researchers, I arrived on their doorstep for my final meeting, bringing a bouquet of flowers and an unsolicited report on the past year, which I had managed to pare down to six pages. I had a happy reunion with Mary when she came to greet me in the lobby. I thought perhaps there'd be another meeting with her and Matt in the session room with the white couch, but that was never mentioned and I did not see the room again.

I sat in Mary's office for a couple of hours and we chatted from time to time while I filled out a sheaf of questionnaires and then clicked responses to the questions on her computer. I noticed that there were different books on top of her cabinet and that some artwork and bulletin board items had changed, but in general everything was still familiar. After I'd finished the paperwork, Mary brought me down the hall for a private talk with Matt.

It was good to see Matt again, too. I congratulated him on his promotion as a full-fledged member of the faculty. Perhaps he was trying to evoke some gravitas with his new beard, but he still looked like the same young, eager, inquisitive Matt to me. He thanked me for participating in the second States of Consciousness study, which had not yet gathered data from all the volunteers. Matt also described some other programs the research team was planning, and the clearances and documentation that would have to be set up in advance.

He had read the one-year report I had emailed before our meeting that morning, and we talked a little about my activities and reflections of the past year. In particular, I cited my new appreciation for physical incarnation. I said, "I am standing by my insight during the psilocybin session that the Light is the true reality and this world is the hallucination. And I was thinking of you the other day when I came upon another metaphor to describe the incredibly convincing illusion that surrounds us: we're living on the holodeck!"

I also took the opportunity to ask Matt what prompted the institution to undertake this unique study on entheogens and spirituality.

"Researchers can carve out their own subject interests in a medical school like Johns Hopkins," he said. "Roland is a leader in the field and could choose to study a wide range of topics. He began this research not because he was asked to, but because of his genuine interest in the reported effects of these substances. He considers it a legitimate area of scientific inquiry and is very interested in the therapeutic potential of these compounds." I couldn't imagine a more thorough and competent team of researchers to address the issue, and hoped their work would earn a serious reconsideration of substances like psilocybin.

I always enjoyed my visits with Matt, but I wanted to be sure to allow time to meet with Roland.

A Goodbye Gift

When I was escorted to Roland's office, I was pleased to see him looking just the same as he had a year before, smiling and sparkling, but without a tie for once. He took his place behind the desk and directed me to the visitor's chair. I barked out the little announcement I had rehearsed for the day: "My name is Maria Estevez, and I have been drug-free for one year!" Roland chuckled and said, "Well, that's the way we want you."

He reviewed with me the written responses to the questionnaire I had filled out in advance, including the section asking whether I would be willing to take hallucinogens again. Referring to his papers, he also asked additional questions to which he wrote my responses. One, in particular, stood out. "If you could have any dose of psilocybin again — which you can't — what would it be?" The high dose, I replied, believing that had occasioned my transcendental experience. But I was especially amused at his emphatic qualification: *"which you can't."*

I had also addressed the issue of taking psilocybin again in the report I had submitted that day. I repeated my contention that it is the conscious openness to the Divine that one seeks, not some psychedelic effect from hallucinogens. But knowing the hallucinogen enabled this, how could I separate the two?

I readily acknowledged I wanted to be in that state again. It seemed reasonable to me that cultures would use such entheogens sacramentally (the perfect description) to achieve this. Yet my theoretical willingness surely was balanced by the fact that I had neither sought nor taken any drug since I had left the research program. I assured Roland that I would not be interested in any substance except an entheogen, and even then only if I could duplicate the protective supervision at Johns

Hopkins. So, without these options available, using such substances becomes a non-issue.

I also talked about my "living souvenir," those energy surges which frightened me during my first psilocybin session and were continuing, though they had diminished both in frequency and intensity. The occasional shudder or jolt was most likely to occur when I was falling asleep or waking, listening to music, or during meditation, and I had come to feel a little affectionate toward them.

Roland and I discussed my activities and insights over the year, as I had described in my report. When I rhapsodized about the privilege of living on the earth, Roland asked, "And how did that come to you?" I really didn't know, I said. It was the coalescence of many reflections that suddenly shifted into focus so clearly that I considered it a distinct revelation. Even such a long time after my experience with psilocybin, I was still making discoveries.

I hesitated to claim too much change or development. I had been able to sustain some of the insights from the psilocybin sessions, but was aware that others eluded me. I could not judge whether I appeared different to an observer. However, Roland said that he did see changes in me since I'd left the program a year before. When I had resumed my art study, I told him, it wasn't a matter of personal ambition or even the call of creativity so much as a clumsy attempt to go out and do something — anything. Roland leaned back in his chair and said, "But you're *teaching*. That's *huge*." It was a hard call between admitting how modest the class was and favorably impressing Roland, but I could understand his view that it was a way of extending my boundaries.

He began his summary and his formal thanks for my

participation. "We have a gift for each of our volunteers completing the program," he said as he ceremoniously offered me a present which he invited me to open. It was a cloth-bound, slip-cased book with the title stamped in gold: *Cleansing the Doors of Perception*. Roland explained that this was one of a special edition that had been commissioned by the Council on Spiritual Practices, a sponsor of the States of Consciousness study. Each was autographed by author Huston Smith himself. In the front, Mary, Matt and Roland had written inscriptions to me, which I told him I would read and savor at home.

I knew the book well, I said. I had first noticed it in Mary's office early in the program, and had bought a paperback copy of my own. Several months later when I could not easily summarize it for a friend, I reread it with more care and made copious notes. I had closed my one-year report to the researchers with a quotation from the last chapter of that very book. After giving up the entheogens, Smith recognized the danger that "the Reality that trumps everything while it is in full view" will fade into a cold and distant memory.[32] I was sad to discover the same thing.

As I was examining the book and looking for Smith's autograph, I glanced over at Roland barely in time to see that he had brought his palms together in front of his face, closing his eyes and touching his fingertips to his forehead as he bowed slightly to me. I was sorry I had not caught the full range of his gesture, that such a beautiful image had nearly slipped away from me, and I thanked him truly in return.

Roland walked me back down the hall to Mary's office. I expressed my gratitude yet again for being accepted into the program, and we all shared a brief embrace. After Roland left, Mary was telling me how much she had learned from the study and that the volunteers had come to seem like family. She escorted me down to the lobby and pushed open the heavy doors to the street, and this time I really was out of options to postpone my departure.

It was rush hour as I pulled out onto the highway with a sense of satisfaction that I had renewed my friendship with the staff and made a contribution to the project. My participation had extraordinarily enriched my life with new knowledge, new perspectives, and a fresh appreciation of the possibilities waiting to be explored.

CHAPTER 11

The Official Version

If this were a film, the landscape would change from summer fields to swirling red and yellow leaves to falling snowflakes as an illustration of passing time. Not just seasons, but years.

After my final meeting with the Johns Hopkins staff, most circumstances of my home and work continued as usual. In January 2010, almost 22 months after my one-year follow-up, volunteers were provided with information on the psilocybin dosages during their sessions. I learned that I had received the high dose first and the medium-high dose second. I had always wondered whether the dramatic differences in my reaction during those sessions was due to the dosage strength or my physical unfamiliarity with the substance; an argument could have been made for either. Psilocybin had been administered to me in a progressive reduction of 30 mg (per 70 kg of body weight), 20 mg, 10 mg, 5 mg, and 0 mg, so I had guessed correctly the sequence of the remaining three sessions, with the placebo last.

It was startling to realize that if I'd received only the high dose, like the volunteers in the first study, I would not have been one of the 60% who had a mystical experience. The distress of my first session would have formed my complete (and negative) judgment of psilocybin. The results of that single encounter would have been the opposite of the glowing review I was able to give the three lower doses in the second study. I remained curious about how I may have reacted to the high dose if I'd received lower doses first and whether I could have experienced "Oneness" with the high dose if the order had been different.

In June 2011 the study's administrators mailed each volunteer a copy of an announcement being posted on the website of one of the study's sponsors, the Council on Spiritual Practices, summarizing the final results of the study. Also enclosed was the article scheduled for online release by the journal *Psychopharmacology*.

The CSP announcement was titled, "Study Probes 'Sacred Mushroom' Chemical." A subhead gave the issue a new slant: "Scientists seek dosage 'sweet spot.' " Roland was quoted, "We wanted to take a methodical look at how [psilocybin's] effects change with dosage. We seem to have found levels of the substance and particular conditions for its use that give a high probability of a profound and beneficial experience, a low enough probability of psychological struggle, and very little risk of any actual harm."

In broad brushstrokes the CSP press release reviewed the study's aims and methodology, which I already knew well. But reading further I found information about the design of the study that the staff had not disclosed. The volunteers had been divided into two groups, receiving either a progressively ascending or descending sequence of psilocybin doses. Besides observing the effects of differing dose strengths, the study's architects had devised an ingenious method to use the sessions for double duty. With this refinement they could also learn if there were an advantage to building up steadily increasing doses or whether it would be more effective to lead off with the full strength of the substance in the first exposure. More detail was provided in the longer article.

The Fine Print

The study findings published in *Psychopharmacology*,[33] also posted on the CSP website, presented seventeen pages of small print with charts and tables that gave the full clinical details. The article stated that the study had been designed to "optimize the potential for positively valued experiences" by providing preparation and a supportive setting so volunteers could focus on their subjective experiences rather than on tasks. It also revealed the intent to compare ascending and descending sequences of doses. None of the primary monitors and only two of the seven assistant monitors were aware of this aspect of the project's experimental design. The single placebo session was scheduled quasi-randomly to obscure the dose sequence to participants and monitors.

When I volunteered I had been told that the four doses of psilocybin would be administered in mixed order. I could only guess at each dose level based on my previous reactions, but it seemed that the dosage decreased each time, with the placebo given in the final session. At the conclusion I thought that perhaps I was the only volunteer who had been assigned a steadily descending series, though I had not been sure about the order of the first two.

Now I read that the administrators observed, "...it appears that having experience with lower doses facilitates the likelihood of having sustained positive effects after a high dose of psilocybin," which suggested that there would be "an advantage of an ascending dose sequence" in therapeutic applications. They clarified that this finding was contrary to some older recommendations of psychotherapists who held that "a single high-dose overwhelming experience was more therapeutic than an approach that began with small doses and gradually increased the dose over successive experiences."

The release added, "… most volunteers in the ascending dose sequence rated the highest dose session (30 mg/70 kg) as the most personally meaningful (67%) and spiritually significant (78%) of the five sessions; in contrast, a smaller proportion of volunteers in the descending sequence rated the highest dose session as most personally meaningful (22%) and spiritually significant (22%)."

I felt not just agreement but a certain vindication, having reached the same conclusion after my own regimen. The staff had not asked for my advice, but I had badgered them several times that it would be kinder to start with the low doses to help volunteers or patients adjust both physically and psychologically.

In this study, the lowest dose was only 5 mg (per 70 kg of body weight) and, the *Psychopharmacology* article stated, even that dose "produced significant subjective, physiological, and observer-rated effects." The low dose had been my "space station," the gentle and natural, but nevertheless distinctive, transition between everyday reality and the upper realms. Volunteers on the descending dosages who received the impact of six times that amount in their initial exposure would seem much more likely to face problems.

Building on the Johns Hopkins original 2006 investigation, this second study verified that psilocybin "can occasion mystical-type experiences having persistent positive effects on attitudes, mood, and behavior.... Considering the rarity of spontaneous mystical experiences, more than 70% of volunteers in the current study had 'complete' mystical experiences." (The report always qualified the word "complete" with quotation marks.) Responses to questionnaires showed that 13 of the 18 volunteers (72%) had experienced a "complete" mystical experience on either the high or medium-high dose, or both of those. At follow-up 14 months later, 94% of those volunteers rated the experience as the single most or among the five most spiritually significant experiences of their life. Most volunteers (89%) also reported positive changes in behavior, corroborated by family members or others.

However, the data showed that instances of fear, anxiety and delusion also increased proportionately with the dosage. Seven of the 18 volunteers had extreme ratings of fear, fear of insanity, or feeling trapped at some time during a session. Six of them had negative reactions during the high dose (but not influenced by the ascending or descending dose sequence) though most of these were of short duration. The session guides managed these occasions effectively, and the distress did not generally affect the rates of "complete" mystical experience, the study found.

The authors inserted a case study of the unnamed volunteer who had the most sustained anxiety during the high dose and the lowest mystical experience rating immediately after the session of all 18 volunteers studied. My heart was in my throat as I realized they were describing what had happened to *me* — my exact conditions and reaction. They added that this volunteer went on to have a "complete" mystical experience with the medium-high dose and rated it "the single most personally meaningful and spiritually significant of her life." It was embarrassing to be cited in a professional paper as having fallen flat on my face, but satisfying both to serve as a caution and to show that someone could rebound from the worst of it.

At the volunteers' 14-month follow-up, the article said, "there were no reports of any non-study use of hallucinogens since study enrollment. All 18 volunteers appeared to continue to be psychiatrically healthy, high-functioning, productive members of society." However, because of the strict physical and psychological screening of volunteers, and the carefully monitored environment of the study, the authors noted that the results could not be generalized to a larger population.

The article outlined the criteria for applicant selection, provided data on the volunteers' physical condition based on cardiovascular measures and monitor ratings, and also described the rationale for the choice of questionnaires completed by volunteers. One chart in the article even provided short quotations from each volunteer describing new attitudes or practices.

Having determined the optimum doses and sequences for favorable physical and psychological response, the researchers expressed confidence that this study would be useful in the design of therapeutic trials with psilocybin. The list of possible applications was lengthy and wide-ranging, starting with the treatment of psychologically distressed cancer patients facing the existential anxiety brought about by their disease. Now with the supporting data firmly established, the prospects for patient treatment must have given the staff cause for great optimism.

CHAPTER 12

A Glance in the Mirror

This account was intended to document my participation in the States of Consciousness Research Project at Johns Hopkins, describing the application procedures and the protocols, giving examples of personal experience during the activity of psilocybin, and showing how the institution evaluates the results. Long-term psychological changes also may occur, but can be more difficult to attribute definitively to having ingested a hallucinogen months or years earlier.

It would be interesting to learn how my psilocybin experiences compared in subject or in physical and emotional intensity with those of other volunteers in the program. I would have loved to meet with them, but the staff resolutely protected their identities. I know only that scattered around the radius of Baltimore there are several dozen others who react to the opening notes of the Vivaldi guitar concerto with the same anticipation. They too will pause when they hear music from the program's soundtrack, transported back to those occasions they will always remember.

The research questionnaires asked whether the moments of transcendence during a psilocybin session were among the most meaningful in one's life. Without doubt they were for me, but I found the entire process of participating in the study an outstanding experience.

With sixteen years of Catholic schooling, I admit that I got a late start in learning discernment and thinking independently, essential factors in my spiritual development. As the States of Consciousness study progressed and my involvement deepened, the researchers began to suspect I was transferring my early esteem for religion to their academic discipline. But instead I was honoring the kindness, integrity, and high standards of the staff. It was a privilege to work with them.

As I had busied myself with routine activities over my lifetime, I always respected my spiritual orientation. I had searched and studied, winnowed and culled, reassessed and combined approaches until I had fashioned a coherent, resilient, and adaptable system of beliefs. I would have concentrated more directly on this if I'd seen an obvious course, but then no doubt I would have missed something else integral to my personal growth.

Anyone who read the same books as I did, made a pilgrimage, and ingested psilocybin would nevertheless have their own unique results. Yet however events and attitudes shape any person's life, the potential to discover our Divine nature resides in each of us. Through our own desire and intention, our heartfelt and persistent yearning, equally striking responses can occur. If there is any lesson here for the seeker it is simply to learn to question, to explore, and to follow personal guidance. And to have enough patience to last forty years.

The culmination of my search came from a source I had never considered when a powerful entheogen briefly opened me to an aspect of God's Presence, the criterion against which all else is measured. I found that when I had been stripped of the knowledge of my home and my work and my surroundings and my body and even my name, what remained was such a calm, natural, and expansive freedom that returning to those familiar things by which I had defined myself became a disappointment.

How odd it seems to need to make such practical, third-dimensional arrangements to enter the numinous, nondimensional Presence. How strange to have to take this action to become aware of the Source from which I constantly originate. No matter how it may have been hidden before, how can I lose sight of its radiance once it has been shown to me? And what recourse do I have when that level of awareness eludes me?

The research staff sympathized with my feelings of loss as the experience faded. They encouraged me to continue my spiritual practices and to love and to serve, working toward a more integrated understanding and way of life. Yet while the vision was still so fresh, it seemed impossible to imagine that I would ever again be content only to chop wood and carry water.

The occasional moments of joy and clarity are precious, but fleeting. No, I cry, everything has been changed! The mere memory of being in the Light is not enough. I want it all back, this very minute — the deep communion of the mystics. I want to be consumed in that fire, not just warmed by the embers. I want to participate in it consciously, to stride into it from my own strength, scoured and purified and shining as my glorious original Self.

Spiritual teachers tell us that our soul is already in that bliss, and it must be true because psilocybin only temporarily opened me to an unfathomable level of Being. What a gift just to know it is possible, to have been aware of it for even an hour! In the poem I had written for the staff, I sought to express my sense of reverence by describing the white couch as "this soft altar." Yet it was also clear that I would have to learn to find my way there again without depending on the vagaries and risks of any extraneous substances.

Discovering that ad "accidentally" and participating in the States of Consciousness Project has now become the gold standard for me. Whenever I think about forcing an issue, I remember the effortlessness, simplicity, and synchronicity with which this opportunity manifested, and it becomes clear that anything appropriate can flow into my life with similar ease.

At best this example can provide only a snapshot of a particular stage of one person's spiritual evolution. In many respects, I do not appear much altered after my experiences in the study. The elements of my personality remain in place — tendencies, preferences, faults, insecurities — when I would have hoped to have a halo around my head and songbirds lighting on my shoulder. The concepts of "emptiness" and "the void" are still a challenge, although I feel a resonance when Bartholomew calls this "the Vastness." Yet the memories of those moments in the Light are my greatest treasure, and I weigh everything against them. I find myself releasing more, desiring less, and better able to accept what I find before me. Guidance has become more clear, and sometimes a personal message even surfaces. Whatever I do not yet understand will be revealed in its own good time. The fierce desire for the transcendent subsides for the moment, and routine plodding resumes. There are plenty of surprises, delights, and useful tasks in my everyday life.

The Psilocybin Reality

I was amazed to find myself in "the same place" on the four occasions when I received psilocybin, as immense and complex as it may be. Except for my rude, overshot entrance with the first dose, I came to recognize that world and gain a certain facility within it, even in those few visits. I moved through similar sensations and hallmarks of entry each time into an alternate reality I could learn to navigate, where communication without words is direct and unambiguous.

Because psilocybin illuminated a very credible and coherent reality, the question arises whether that is the ever-present foundation of my being or only one of many realities through which the Divine expresses itself. I learned that it can provide inspiration and support, but can also mirror back whatever error, inaccuracy, or negativity one brings to it. The staff had cautioned that I could not assume that subsequent sessions with psilocybin would not bring fear or confrontation.

A variety of altered states seems to be possible because other drugs and natural experiences are said to produce different effects. Some persons taking hallucinogens have reported bright colors and jewels, none of which I have seen. The realms I explored during the activity of psilocybin impressed me as the true reality, or at least *a* true reality. From that perspective, the *physical* world is the illusion, and anyone who previously had been deceived into believing that alone is "real" would be embarrassed. The knowledge that I discovered through the action of psilocybin was compelling and convincing, but perhaps it is only one kind of knowing.

This information and insight, however, has a considerable advantage in determining my conscious decisions and actions because it was absorbed at such a primal level. It came as direct experience, impressed on me in a most immediate and intimate manner — not from conventional instruction, investigation, assumption, or consensus. One does not argue with this apprehension of reality.

Some observers, especially those in a religious framework, have doubts that a mystical experience occasioned by hallucinogens can be the same as one occurring spontaneously. But no one who has not had both kinds is in a position to compare, including me, and there are varieties and degrees of each. Whatever the impetus, such an experience will elevate and transform the individual's thought and action and, through these, continually ripple outward.

The entheogens may provide invaluable access, but no matter how we reach that understanding, I am quite sure that we are still that perfect Light at our core. For so long we have been taught that human nature is weak, flawed, and unworthy. We are seldom reminded that this Light is not something to be earned or granted but is the definition of our very selves.

I have no means to verify this, but perhaps the phrase given to me, "Once the door is opened, it will never again be completely closed," applies to our basic cellular structure as well as to the spiritual impulse. Once that channel has been seared through the brain and body by the entheogen, the physical and psychic paths remain like shining streaks through the wilderness of all that lies beyond the familiar. Whenever we dare to venture beyond the psychological fortress we have constructed to circumscribe and define ourselves, vestiges of the experience offer signposts to guide us. Some indelible memory stirs and reawakens our anticipation, our confidence, our knowing. We are capable, secure in our being, and our expansion takes on a gentle and natural quality.

After my first dose of psilocybin, I interpreted my body's message "I did it for you" as a gesture of submission and sacrifice to enable the mind and spirit to reach their own fulfillment. But in time I came to see that the phrase also could mean, "This body has accepted its own initiation, a voluntary transformation, so that conscious access now will be available more directly. The connection has been established. Use it."

I considered my psilocybin experiences in view of what I had learned about the processes of consciousness. One primary principle is that we can experience only what we permit within our personal belief system. Examining my perceptions of God as evidence of existing beliefs, then, it was consistent to find Him to be intelligent and glorious, omnipotent, loving and joyful — qualities I already associated with the deity, whether my level of comprehension was formed by standard religious doctrines, by information from other spiritual traditions or channeled sources, or my own halting contemplations of the infinite. I would have added too, even before my transcendental experience in the second session, my belief that God would be formless but would be perceived as Light in any physical context.

As convincing and as moving as that encounter was, it did still mirror my expectations. Was this the personification of my preconceptions, an outpicturing of God in the abstract terms I was already comfortable with after years of religious and metaphysical readings and reflections, or did I tap into an Absolute Source described by the mystics? I have no way to be sure how my beliefs may have influenced the vision, but the deep, moving impression remains.

I could be persuaded that during the action of psilocybin, especially with the lower doses, the voyager would encounter emotions and images drawn from his own mindset, but the higher doses catapult one far beyond the capacity of reason and imagination. The conventional definition of ego has no place in those realms, but not because we are suddenly enabled to master it, to intentionally surrender it, or to choose to step beyond it. In the all-consuming Presence, the ego simply falls away by itself.

If we are not only created in His image and likeness but verily *made* of God-stuff, an aspect of the infinite temporarily taking form, then what we see in a mystical experience is but a glance in the mirror. We are dazzled by our own greater selves. We are *all* amazing. Just as we can hide an "I love you" note in someone's pocket, God can hide one in a mushroom. Or rather, perhaps we are leaving a message for ourselves saying, "Remember who you are."

Native traditions have long acknowledged "plant teachers" such as mushrooms for their singular properties. While some people experience a sense of communion with God during the activity of entheogens, others find varying degrees of openness, participation, and emotional response, depending on their dosage and disposition.

I am not advocating that spiritual seekers experiment with hallucinogens. I am qualified to do no more than relate my own stories, and to provide a vivid illustration that psilocybin can cause fearful as well as ecstatic reactions. But new studies at Johns Hopkins and other institutions make a persuasive case for reassessment of such substances with appropriate respect for their potential to transform. With proper preparation and supervision, such agents can gently free the personality from its customary boundaries to explore a new perspective and discover a wider range of responses.

During my strong first dose of psilocybin, I worried that I would never return to the self-definition I knew. Like a released bird hurrying back to its cage, I was intimidated by that strange realm, and sought the security of the known. Now when I consider the limitations of this reality I find myself yearning to explore again the dimensions that once caused me such fear. I have been reassured and encouraged by those journeys, and will remain forever changed by them.

The transcendental state revealed my original being, ever-present even when I cannot perceive it. I will reestablish my conscious link to that again, though perhaps not before the end of this life, and I appreciate even more the benefits of progressing in organic, incremental steps. It is a consolation when Tolle says that once the process of awakening and return has begun, it is irreversible.[34]

The issues now coming to my attention are broader in scope than before, and not only because of what I experienced through participation in this project. The range of spiritual subjects, and public forums for learning and sharing, have grown exponentially in recent years, a boon for every seeker. The world still endures vicious religious conflicts, and every culture has its shadow of fear and prejudice. But metaphysical principles I once had to research and work to comprehend are now widely known and accepted. Truths once whispered only in mystery schools are broadcast to millions.

Instead of musty scholastic debates about how many angels can dance on the head of a pin, we now earnestly discuss mankind's role in the planet's stewardship, the importance of living in the present moment, and the perception of God as life and consciousness itself. In addition to copious new information, it is said that greater energies are becoming available to us as well. The collective heart is opening, the pace is quickening. As promised to the individual, when certain levels are reached by the group there is no turning back.

My answer would still be yes if I were asked, "Do you believe that God is everywhere?" I also have come to believe that communion with God does not depend on bread or wine, or even on entheogens. It is ours by nature, the life force that expresses as our personal identities and permeates every point in the universe. Bringing this into the forefront of our awareness — recognizing it, examining it, exploring it, testing it, assimilating it, falling into it, reveling in it, and being joyously overwhelmed by its utter improbability — that is the task, and the invitation.

Even as each of us learns to align with the Divine, however we may conceive it, science is developing ways to deliver us to the gates of heaven more reliably than ever before. I was honored to be a part of this thorough and respectful research, and with its assistance to have experienced the most extraordinary event of my life.

It happened on a Tuesday morning, on the third floor of an office building in Baltimore.

BOOKS: MY TOP SHELF

APPENDICES

NOTES

Books: My Top Shelf

These are my best friends, the titles that have sifted to the top shelf of my spiritual library. I return to these favorites again and again both for inspiration and information. Relaxing into their company for a visit, I am restored and invigorated.

Some of these books are channeled, meaning the writer attunes to a message from a spirit entity or receives direct dictation, sometimes in trance. The material varies as widely as that of human authors and arguably deserves the same consideration. It has the potential to be a rich source of knowledge for a discerning reader, and reviewing it impartially will sharpen our capacity to make personal judgments.

BARTHOLOMEW, channeled by Mary-Margaret Moore from 1977 to 1995, is as lucid and loving a teacher as I have encountered in person or in print. Four books of his edited group lectures are available, plus a fifth in which he is quoted extensively. Bartholomew continually urges the reader forward with expansive visions, emphasizing personal power and exploring the deepest spiritual subjects in clear, contemporary language.

I Come as a Brother
From the Heart of a Gentle Brother
Reflections of an Elder Brother
Planetary Brother
Journeys With a Brother

SETH describes himself as "an entity no longer focused in physical reality." He was channeled through the late Jane Roberts who also authored books on her own. Beginning in the 1970s when Jane and her husband came to accept Seth's authenticity, this copious material provided a detailed and consistent framework to explain the physical universe and our untapped abilities. Seth's best-known books are:

The Seth Material
Seth Speaks
The Nature of Personal Reality

JOEL GOLDSMITH began his healing and teaching ministry around 1930. His tone can sound old-fashioned and repetitious to modern sensibilities, but he conveys a deep level of understanding and provides timeless lessons. Each of his books, despite its specific title, can be counted on to address all of his recurring themes such as oneness, healing, abundance, and meditation, for he appreciates all of them as different aspects of God. These are representative of his prolific work:

The Infinite Way
Invisible Supply
Living Between Two Worlds
The Thunder of Silence
A Parenthesis in Eternity

DAVID SPANGLER, an American who has characterized himself as a "practical mystic," served for several years as co-director of the Findhorn community in northern Scotland soon after its founding in the early 1970s. As a natural sensitive he has offered some channeled material, but usually writes and speaks in his own voice. He now resides in the Seattle area with his family, teaching and publishing through the Lorian Association. Spangler's work concentrates on an approach he has named Incarnational Spirituality. Some of his titles include:

> *Apprenticed to Spirit*
> *Reflections on the Christ*
> *Subtle Worlds*

OTHER BOOKS. These are some other books that have contributed to my understanding and which I can recommend.

> *The Power of Now*, by Eckhart Tolle
> *A New Earth*, by Eckhart Tolle
> *Conscious Life*, by Ramon Stevens
> *Emmanuel's Book*, series by Pat Rodegast
> *Conversations With God*, series by Neale Donald Walsch
> *Freedom From the Known*, by Krishnamurti
> *Awakening*, by Pir Vilayat Inayat Khan
> *Energy Medicine*, by Donna Eden

APPENDIX I

Press Release July 11, 2006, at *www.hopkinsmedicine.org*

Hopkins Scientists Show Hallucinogen in Mushrooms Creates Universal "Mystical" Experience

Rigorous study hailed as landmark

Using unusually rigorous scientific conditions and measures, Johns Hopkins researchers have shown that the active agent in "sacred mushrooms" can induce mystical/spiritual experiences descriptively identical to spontaneous ones people have reported for centuries.

The resulting experiences apparently prompt positive changes in behavior and attitude that last several months, at least.

The agent, a plant alkaloid called psilocybin, mimics the effect of serotonin on brain receptors — as do some other hallucinogens — but precisely where in the brain and in what manner are unknown.

An account of the study, accompanied by an editorial and four experts' commentaries, appears online today in the journal *Psychopharmacology*.

Cited as "landmark" in the commentary by former National Institute on Drug Abuse (NIDA) director, Charles Schuster, the research marks a new systematic approach to studying certain hallucinogenic compounds that, in the 1950s, showed signs of therapeutic potential or value in research into the nature of consciousness and sensory perception. "Human consciousness... is a function of the ebb and flow of neural impulses in various regions of the brain — the very substrate that drugs such as psilocybin act upon," Schuster says. "Understanding what mediates these effects is clearly within the realm of neuroscience and deserves investigation."

"A vast gap exists between what we know of these drugs — mostly from descriptive anthropology — and what we believe we can understand using modern clinical pharmacology techniques," says study leader Roland Griffiths, Ph.D., a professor with Hopkins' departments of Neuroscience and Psychiatry and Behavioral Biology. "That gap is large because, as a reaction to the excesses of the 1960s, human research with hallucinogens has been basically frozen in time these last forty years."

All of the study's authors caution about substantial risks of taking psilocybin under conditions not appropriately supervised. "Even in this study, where we greatly controlled conditions to minimize adverse effects, about a third of subjects reported significant fear, with some also reporting transient feelings of paranoia," says Griffiths. "Under unmonitored conditions, it's not hard to imagine those emotions escalating to panic and dangerous behavior."

The researchers' message isn't just that psilocybin can produce mystical experiences. "I had a healthy skepticism going into this," says Griffiths, "and that finding alone was a surprise." But, as important, he says, "is that, under very defined conditions, with careful preparation, you can safely and fairly reliably occasion what's called a primary mystical experience that may lead to positive changes in a person. It's an early step in what we hope will be a large body of scientific work that will ultimately help people."

The authors acknowledge the unusual nature of the work, treading, as it does, a fine line between neuroscience and areas most would consider outside science's realm. "But establishing the basic science here is necessary," says Griffiths, "to take advantage of the possible benefits psilocybin can bring to our understanding of how thought, emotion, and ultimately behavior are grounded in biology."

Griffiths is quick to emphasize the scientific intent of the study. "We're just measuring what can be observed," he says; "We're not entering into 'Does God exist or not exist.' This work can't and won't go there."

In the study, more than 60 percent of subjects described the effects of psilocybin in ways that met criteria for a "full mystical experience" as measured by established psychological scales. One third said the experience was the single most spiritually significant of their lifetimes; and more than two-thirds rated it among their five most meaningful and spiritually significant. Griffiths says subjects liken it to the importance of the birth of their first child or the death of a parent.

Two months later, 79 percent of subjects reported moderately or greatly increased well-being or life satisfaction compared with those given a placebo at the same test session. A majority said their mood, attitudes and behaviors had changed for the better. Structured interviews with family members, friends and co-workers generally confirmed the subjects' remarks. Results of a year-long followup are being readied for publication.

Psychological tests and subjects' own reports showed no harm to study participants, though some admitted extreme anxiety or other unpleasant effects in the hours following the psilocybin capsule. The drug has not been observed to be addictive or physically toxic in animal studies or human populations. "In this regard," says Griffiths, a psychopharmacologist, "it contrasts with MDMA (ecstasy), amphetamines or alcohol."

The study isn't the first with psilocybin, the researchers say, though some of the earlier ones, done elsewhere, had notably less rigorous design, were less thorough in measuring outcomes or lacked longer-term follow-up.

In the present work, 36 healthy, well-educated volunteers — most of them middle-aged — with no family history of psychosis or bipolar disorder were selected. All had active spiritual practices. "We thought a familiarity with spiritual practice would give them a framework for interpreting their experiences and that they'd be less likely to be confused or troubled by them," Griffiths says. All gave informed consent to the study approved by Hopkins' institutional review board.

Each of thirty of the subjects attended two separate 8-hour drug sessions, at two month intervals. On one they received psilocybin, on another, methylphenidate (Ritalin), the active placebo.

In designing the study, researchers had to overcome or at least, greatly minimize two hurdles: the risk of adverse side-effects and the likelihood that the expectations of getting the test drug or the placebo would influence subjects' perceptions.

To lessen the former, each subject met several times, before drug sessions began, with a reassuring "monitor," a medical professional experienced in observing drug study participants. Monitors stayed with them during the capsule-taking sessions. Actual trials took place in a room outfitted like a comfortable, slightly upscale living room, with soft music and indirect, non-laboratory lighting. Heart rate and blood pressure were measured throughout.

The researchers countered "expectancy" by having both monitors and subjects "blinded" to what substance would be given. For ethical reasons, subjects were told about hallucinogens' possible effects, but also learned they could, instead, get other substances — weak or strong — that might change perception or consciousness. Most important, a third "red herring" group of six subjects had two blinded placebo sessions, then were told they'd receive psilocybin at a third. This tactic — questionnaires later verified — kept participants and monitors in the dark at the first two sessions about each capsule's contents.

Nine established questionnaires and a new, specially created followup survey were used to rate experiences at appropriate times in the study. They included those that differentiate effects of psychoactive drugs, that detect altered states of consciousness, that rate mystical experiences and assess changes in outlook.

The study, Griffiths adds, has advanced understanding of hallucinogen abuse.

As for where the work could lead, the team is planning a trial of patients suffering from advanced cancer-related depression or anxiety, following up suggestive research several decades ago. They're also designing studies to test a role for psilocybin in treating drug dependence.

The study was funded by grants from NIDA and the Council on Spiritual Practices.

Una McCann, M.D., William Richards, Ph.D., of the Johns Hopkins Medical Institutions and Robert Jesse of the Council on Spiritual Practices, San Francisco, were co-researchers.

The commentaries on this study that appear in this issue of *Psychopharmacology* are available at:
www.hopkinsmedicine.org/Press_releases/2006/GriffithsCommentaries.pdf
and include remarks by:

Hopkins neuroscientist and Professor of Neuroscience, Solomon Snyder, M.D.

Former NIDA head Charles Schuster, Ph.D., now Distinguished Professor of Psychiatry and Behavioral Neuroscience at the Wayne State University School of Medicine

Herbert Kleber, M.D., a professor of psychiatry at Columbia University and a former deputy director of the White House Office of National Drug Control Policy (ONDCP)

David Nichols, Ph.D., with the Purdue University School of Pharmacy and Pharmaceutical Sciences

Harriet de Wit, Ph.D., at the University of Chicago Department of Psychiatry. DeWit is the editor of *Psychopharmacology*.

APPENDIX II

www.hopkinsmedicine.org
July 11, 2006

The following Q&A is with Roland Griffiths, the study's lead researcher.

Q 1: *Why did you undertake this research?*
In the 1950s and 1960s, basic science and applied research studies were taking place with hallucinogens, offering hints that they might be of value in psychotherapy, addiction treatment, and creativity enhancement, and suggestions that the hallucinogens can occasion mystical-type experiences. Laws enacted in response to excesses of the "psychedelic 1960s" stopped almost all that work, leaving some promising threads dangling. Despite ongoing illicit and licit use, remarkably little is known, from the standpoint of modern psycho-pharmacology research, about the acute and long-term effects of the hallucinogens. Our study is among the first to re-open this field. Since the Hopkins psilocybin work began, researchers at other major universities, such as UCLA, the University of Arizona, and Harvard, have begun planning or are carrying out hallucinogen research.

Q 2: *Do you have any sign that the same brain "machinery" affected by psilocybin is identical to what people experience in spiritual epiphanies that occur without drugs?*
That work hasn't been done yet, though there is good reason to believe that similar mechanisms are at work during profound religious experiences, however they might be occasioned (for example, by fasting, meditation, controlled breathing, sleep deprivation, near death experiences, infectious disease states, or psychoactive substances such as psilocybin). The neurology of religious experience, newly termed neurotheology, is drawing interest as a new frontier of study.

Q 3: *Is this God in a pill? Does it render God or "revelation" irrelevant?*

The scientific method works with what can be observed in the physical realm, using tools such as atomic particle detectors, medical imaging devices, people's responses to psychological tests, interviews, and behavioral observations. We are attempting neither to validate nor to invalidate the truth of claims that some people have made about metaphysical realities as a consequence of their psilocybin experiences (or as a consequence of their meditation, fasting, or prayer experiences) — that's beyond our purview as scientists. It is within the purview of science to study the changes in mood, values, view of self, and behaviors that may follow such experiences.

Of course it would be a profound mistake to confuse the experience of something for the thing itself. We are not aware of study participants who felt their psilocybin experience devalued their own religious traditions; interviews suggested the opposite was more usually the case.

Q 4: *Are you trying to find a short cut to the spiritual journey that some people pursue for years?*

Our focus in this research was to study the effects of psilocybin using the methods of modern psychopharmacology. It's true that "transformative" changes in values, self-perception, and behaviors have been reported across cultures and eras as a consequence of mystical-type experience. This bears investigation.

Q 5: *Should religions feel threatened by this work?*

I can't see why.

The psychologist Walter Clark, in his 1958 book *The Psychology of Religion*, had this to say: "There is no more difficult word to define than 'religion'...With full recognition that we are on ground where the experts disagree ... we will venture our own definition. It is our feeling that religion can be most characteristically described as the inner experience of the individual when he senses a Beyond, especially as evidenced by the effect of this experience on his behavior when he actively attempts to harmonize his life with the Beyond."

Many of the volunteers in our study reported, in one way or another, a direct, personal experience of the "Beyond." Far from being threatened, the only thing we can imagine being of greater interest to religions is whether people live more wholesome, compassionate, and equanimous lives in consequence of such experiences.

Q 6: *Why did you use volunteers who have active spiritual practices? Didn't that help assure the results you got?*

Psilocybin and similar compounds have been reported to sometimes bring about experiences called spiritual, religious, mystical, visionary, revelatory, etc. Such experiences may be difficult psychologically and emotionally. We felt that volunteers who had some engagement with prayer, meditation, churchgoing, or similar activities would be better equipped to understand and consolidate any mystical-type experiences they might have in the study.

Q 7: *Aren't hallucinogens dangerous? How can you give them to human volunteers?*

No mind-affecting drug is absolutely safe. But the risks of the hallucinogens can be managed in appropriate research settings. Unlike drugs of abuse such as alcohol and cocaine, the classic hallucinogens are not known to be physically toxic and they are virtually non-addictive, so those are not concerns.

The primary effect of psilocybin, in medium to large doses, is strong alteration of consciousness. It is possible that such experiences can trigger latent schizophrenia in susceptible individuals. Thus in our study we disqualified potential volunteers whose personal or family psychiatric histories indicate that they may be at increased risk of that disorder.

Our study confirms that some individuals, during some or all of the hours of the drug's action, may experience paranoia, extreme anxiety, or other unpleasant psychological effects. It is not difficult to imagine such stresses leading to dangerous or inappropriate behaviors, which may constitute the substance's most prominent risk. We managed that in our study through a short course of psychological preparation and through careful and interpersonally sensitive monitoring of each drug session. The monitors were trained to provide reassurance (e.g., supportive words or gentle touch to a hand) if needed.

Q 8: *What kind of substance is psilocybin?*

Psilocybin is one of a class of compounds whose primary activity is known to be on 5-HT-2a/c serotonin receptors. Their effects include changes in perception and cognition. In the pharmacology literature, this class of drugs is called "hallucinogens," though they rarely cause "hallucinations" in the sense of seeing or hearing things that are not there. Within other academic fields, the term 'entheogen,' roughly meaning "spirit-facilitating," is coming into prominence for this class of substances.

Q 9: *Studies at Hopkins have shown the potential for brain damage from MDMA ("ecstasy"). How do you know psilocybin doesn't have the same risk?*

Some studies have shown that MDMA can damage certain nerve cells. There is no experimental or clinical evidence in animals or humans that psilocybin, even in very high doses, is similarly neuro-toxic. Enough research has been done with psilocybin, starting in the 1950s, that we can be reasonably confident that it is not physically toxic in doses humans ordinarily use. This is consistent with the fact that psilocybin-containing mushrooms have not, in millennia of use, acquired a reputation of being physically harmful. Traditions that use psilocybin mushrooms do, however, caution about psychological and spiritual risks of using them haphazardly.

Q 10: *Isn't your work similar to what Timothy Leary did?*

We are conducting rigorous, systematic research with psilocybin under carefully monitored conditions, a route which Dr. Leary abandoned in the early 1960s.

Q 11: *Isn't there a risk that a study like this could encourage abuse of psilocybin or similar substances?*

Our report explains the substantial risks that could easily follow from use without the psychiatric screening, preparation, and monitoring we provided in this study.

Herbert D. Kleber, M.D., addressed this question in a commentary published concurrently with our paper. Dr. Kleber is Professor of Psychiatry at the Columbia University College of Physicians & Surgeons and the Director of Division on Substance Abuse of the New York State Psychiatric Institute. He previously served as a deputy director of the White House Office of National Drug Control Policy (ONDCP).

Dr. Kleber wrote, "The positive findings of the study cannot help but raise concern in some that it will lead to increased experimenting with these substances by youth in the kind of uncontrolled and unmonitored fashion that produced casualties over the past three decades...

"Any study reporting a positive or useful effect of a drug of abuse raises these same concerns. In this Internet age, however, where youth are deluged with glowing personal reports in chat rooms and web sites as well as detailed information about the various agents and how to use them, it is less likely that a scientific study would move the needle much.

"Psychedelic drug use has remained in a relatively constant range over the past three decades as various fads have come and gone and enthusiastic personal accounts are balanced by negative reports about casualties.

Discovering how these mystical and altered consciousness states arise in the brain could have major therapeutic possibilities, e.g., treatment of intolerable pain, treatment of refractory depression, amelioration of the pain and suffering of the terminally ill, to name but a few, as well as the... needed improvement in treatment of substance abuse... so that it would be scientifically shortsighted not to pursue them."

Huston Smith comments

Huston Smith, holder of 12 honorary degrees, is one of the great authorities on comparative religion. His book *The World's Religions* has for forty years been the most widely used textbook on its subject, and in 1996 he was the focus of a five part Bill Moyers PBS program, "The Wisdom of Faith with Huston Smith." See *hustonsmith.net* for more.

Commenting on the Griffiths et al. study, Smith said: "Mystical experience seems to be as old as humankind, forming the core of many if not all of the great religious traditions. Some ancient cultures, such as classical Greece, and some contemporary small-scale cultures, have made use of psychoactive plants and chemicals to occasion such experiences. But this is the first scientific demonstration in 40 years, and the most rigorous ever, that profound mystical states can be produced safely in the laboratory. The potential is great."

Smith also issued a caution and suggested that further research on the topic include social as well as neurological variables: "In the end, it's altered traits, not altered states, that matter. 'By their fruits shall ye know them.' It's good to learn that volunteers having even this limited experience had lasting benefits. But human history suggests that without a social vessel to hold the wine of revelation, it tends to dribble away. In most cases, even the most extraordinary experiences provide lasting benefits to those who undergo them and people around them only if they become the basis of ongoing work. That's the next research question, it seems to me: What conditions of community and practice best help people to hold on to what comes to them in those moments of revelation, converting it into abiding light in their own lives?" ■

Notes

1. David Brown, "Drug's Mystical Properties Confirmed," *The Washington Post*, July 11, 2006, A8.

2. Mary-Margaret Moore, *From the Heart of a Gentle Brother* (Taos, NM: High Mesa Press, 1987), 7.

3. Jane Roberts, *Seth Speaks: The Eternal Validity of the Soul* (San Rafael, CA: Amber-Allen Publishing, 1972), 227.

4. William Blake, *The Marriage of Heaven and Hell* (New York: Dover Publications, Inc., 1994), 36.

5. Huston Smith, *Cleansing the Doors of Perception* (New York: J.P. Tarcher/Penguin Putnam, 2000), 130.

6. Matt. 7:9 (American Standard Version)

7. Mary-Margaret Moore, *Reflections of an Elder Brother* (Taos, NM: High Mesa Press, 1989), 38.

8. Mary-Margaret Moore, *From the Heart of a Gentle Brother* (Taos, NM: High Mesa Press, 1987), 24-25.

9. Barbara Ann Brennan, *Light Emerging: The Journey of Personal Healing* (New York, Bantam Books, 1993) 288-289.

10. Gable, R.S. (1993). Toward a comparative overview of dependence potential and acute toxicity of psychoactive substances used nonmedically. *Am. J. Drug Alcohol Abuse, 19*, 263-281.

11. Jane Roberts, *The Seth Material* (Manhasset, NY: New Awareness Network Inc., 1970), 245.

12. Pir Vilayat Inayat Khan, *Awakening: A Sufi Experience* (New York: Jeremy P. Tarcher/Putnam, 1999), 19.

13. Mary-Margaret Moore, *Reflections of an Elder Brother* (Taos, NM: High Mesa Press, 1989), 69.

14. Aldous Huxley, *The Doors of Perception* (New York: Harper & Row, Publishers, Inc., 1954), 79.

15. William Wordsworth, "The World Is Too Much with Us," (*A Treasury of Great Poems*, Louis Untermeyer, ed., New York: Simon and Schuster, Inc., 1942) 650.

16. Rudolf Steiner, *The Archangel Michael: His Mission and Ours*. (Hudson, NY: Anthroposophic Press, 1994), 234-235.

17. Ibid., 287.

18. Ibid., 53-60.

19. Mary-Margaret Moore, *From the Heart of a Gentle Brother* (Taos, NM: High Mesa Press, 1987), 146.

20. Mary-Margaret Moore, *Planetary Brother* (Taos, NM: High Mesa Press, 1991), 111-118.

21. Jane Roberts, *The Nature of Personal Reality* (San Rafael, CA: Amber-Allen Publishing, 1974), 163-178.

22. Alan Watts, *The Joyous Cosmology: Adventures in the Chemistry of Consciousness* (New York: Pantheon Books, 1970), 26.

23. Jane Roberts, *The Seth Material* (Manhasset, NY: New Awareness Network Inc., 1970), 40.

24. Ezra Pound, "The Ballad of the Goodly Fere" (*A Treasury of Great Poems*, Louis Untermeyer, ed., New York: Simon and Schuster, Inc., 1942) 1127-1129.

25. Jane Roberts, *Seth Speaks: The Eternal Validity of the Soul* (San Rafael, CA: Amber-Allen Publishing, 1972), 54-55.

26. Huston Smith, *Cleansing the Doors of Perception* (Boulder, CO: Sentient Publications, 2003), 153.

27. Eckhart Tolle, *The Power of Now* (Novato, CA: New World Library, 1999), 118.

28. Joel Goldsmith, *Living Between Two Worlds* (Austell, GA: I-Level Publications, 1974) 25.

29. Joel Goldsmith, *Invisible Supply* (New York: HarperCollins Publishers, 1994), 34.

30. Jane Roberts, *Seth Speaks: The Eternal Validity of the Soul* (San Rafael, CA: Amber-Allen Publishing, 1972), 44.

31. Mary-Margaret Moore, *From the Heart of a Gentle Brother* (Taos, NM: High Mesa Press, 1987), 172-173.

32. Huston Smith, *Cleansing the Doors of Perception* (Boulder, CO: Sentient Publications, 2003), 131.

33. Griffiths, R.R., Johnson, M.W., Richards, W.A., Richards, B.D., McCann, U., Jesse, R. (2011). Psilocybin occasioned mystical-type experiences: Immediate and persisting dose-related effects. *Psychopharmacology, 218,* 649-65.

34. Eckhart Tolle, *A New Earth* (New York: Dutton, 2005), 7.